IN THE ROOM OF
PERSISTENT SORRY: ESSAYS

Kristina Marie Darling

C&R Press
Conscious & Responsible

Printed in the United States of America

First Edition
1 2 3 4 5 6 7 8 9

Cover art by Eugenia Loli
Cover design by C&R Press
Interior design by Rachel Kelli and Jojo Rita
Copyright ©2019 Kristina Marie Darling

ISBN 978-1-936196-91-3
Library of Congress Control Number 2018956120

C&R Press
Conscious & Responsible
crpress.org

For special discounted bulk purchases, please contact:
C&R Press sales@crpress.org
Contact info@crpress.org to book events, readings and author signings.

Contents

"THE NATURAL LANGUAGE OF ARCHITECTURE":
NOTES ON THE DOMESTIC SUBLIME

IN A RECENT ESSAY, VIRGINIA KONCHAN DESCRIBES the domestic sublime as "a song of praise" that takes one's "dual identity," that push and pull between public and private spaces, as its subject. Indeed, to enter "the house of our childhood," with its "nooks and garrets and stairs and passages," is to witness the self as it is made strange, to see the public persona one remembers so clearly held at a distance. When one praises this divide, one is singing of the otherness that is contained within the self, finding beauty in the instability inherent in one's own identity.

Three recent experimental texts pay homage to this duality, this dividedness with subtlety and grace. Lisa Robertson's *Occasional Work and Seven Walks from the Office for Soft Architecture,* Catherine Theis's *Medea,* and John Beer's *Lucinda* praise the movement between architectural spaces, and between selves, while at the same time calling attention to the problems this poses for a conventional understanding of voice, identity, and memory. Though vastly different in style and approach, these three collections present voice, and the self it embodies, as a performance of the spaces we inhabit, or, more specifically, their buried histories, narratives, and politics.

In many ways, this idea of voice as a performance, as an interpretation of architectural space, is enacted most visibly in these writers' representations of femininity. While ranging from verse plays to enjambed lines, hybrid forms, and gratifyingly dense essays, these beautifully rendered texts are driven by an interest in the ways that "narrow scaffolds" and "stolen engravings" can give rise to artifice, that visible girlishness which "blooms in tandem with decay."

*   *   *

1

Catherine Theis' *Medea* posits voice as an architecture in itself, a carefully decorated room within the room that the speaker inhabits. Though taking the form of a verse play, and framed as a creative translation of the original text, Theis offers her own unique vocabulary of imagery to accompany the heroine's descent into a broken marriage, substance abuse, and despair. As the book unfolds, the "white flowers" and "vases of irises" that surround Medea elicit vastly different soliloquies and conversations, all of which offer insight into different facts of both her character and the narrative that it gives rise to.

For instance, Medea's dialogue section when "near the tennis courts of a neighborhood park" considers the self-censorship and erasure of voice that the suburbs, and their implicit gender politics, gives rise to,

> **I'm dead serious** ~~when I say all I want to do is drink beer and eat stinky cheese that smells and~~ **looks like dead matter** ~~from inside an old man's nose until my middle bloats [...]~~

Though Medea's soliloquy reads as an interrogation of the space she inhabits, the Theis' use of form ultimately complicates what might otherwise have been construed as a simple argument. In many ways, Theis' use of strikethrough subtly and powerfully evokes the fact that architectural spaces give rise to erasure – of voices, of selves, and of possibilities. The gentrified setting ultimately determines what cannot, and will not ever, be spoken. Additionally, the fragments of language we are left with ("I'm dead serious" and "looks like dead matter") do not fit together neatly, grammatically or narratively speaking. The incongruousness of these fragments, their ill-fitting clauses, speaks to the contradictions inherent in this dividedness, the difficulty of inhabiting an identity that is so entirely changeable.

As the play unfolds, this problem – of the self and its instability as it passes through "coffee shops," "bars" and "libraries" – is revealed as an inexorable part of the female condition. In the Scene One of the Fourth Movement of the play, Media traipses through a "kitchen," replete with "a large sign above the sink. It reads: If you dirty a dish / You wash that fish / Off the plate or else!" Here we witness Media attempting to reclaim the domestic, not as a space of labor, but one of collaboration and partnership. When she speaks, what seems like a performance, and subversion, of the implicit politics of the domestic becomes less clear-cut,

> Prevention better than tragedy?
> Is that even possible?
> I'd rather be an atomic flower.
> Pretty, but self-imploding.

Theis, through Medea's provocative metaphor of the "atomic flower," calls our attention to the violence inherent in the domestic. The female protagonist must inhabit a space that is historically one of disempowerment, performing the function the space demands while at the same reclaiming agency among the "pink napkins" and "embroidery" that surrounds her. In many ways, this "pretty, but self-imploding" vision of womanhood represents a kind of identity in which this implicit violence, this dividedness, is internalized. What's more, one reclaims agency while at the same time questioning its permanence, especially as one shifts between rooms and buildings. As Media herself asks moments later, "Are you still listening to me?"

*   *   *

Beer's *Lucinda* complicates Theis' exploration of voice as an interpretation, and an enactment, of the architectural spaces we inhabit. Though drifting from verse to prose, dramatic writing, and hybrid forms, this innovative text is unified by its abiding interest in the moments of incongruity, that refusal to perform a particular role when prompted. As the work unfolds, Beer embraces and interrogates this disconnect, that luminous aperture between oneself and the version of oneself demanded by a particular context.   In many ways, Beer's approach to identity and voice gives rise to a much larger question, a consideration of whether there exists an identity core, a self that persists even as we pass from room to room.

Beer writes, for example, midway through *Lucinda*,

> Joey: I guess one difference would be that poets write poems. I mean, I write poems. I don't write philosophy.
>
> Ross & Rachel: Joey!
>
> Joey: I'm just saying. I'm curious. I'm a curious person.
>
> Chandler: You are indeed, buddy.
>
> Phoebe: CHAOS WAITS FOR THE TOUCH OF LOVE TO UNFOLD AS A HARMONIOUS WHOLE! Wait, did I say that out loud?
>
> All others: Uh-huh.

Beer immediately calls our attention to the disconnect between mass culture, a setting derived from the most widely circulated text of its oeuvre, and the texture of the language presented within that seemingly superficial context.   He subtly and skillfully suggests that it is the setting, that familiar and widely televised apartment, that renders the language not only strange, but entirely inappropriate. What's more, by enlisting the cast of *Friends* to discuss the boundaries of poetry and philosophy, and forcing them to transition between lyrical and colloquial language, Beer evokes the interstitial space between self and performance.

In many ways, this notion of an identity buried beneath what is visible to the world comes across through most powerfully in Phoebe's dialogue section, with those the wildly metaphorical lines she does realize she has spoken aloud. Beer asks us to consider what is withheld as a result of architectural spaces, their implicit boundaries and politics. He reminds us of that identity and silence are inevitably, inextricably bound together.

What that in mind, Beer reminds us that this space between thought and speech is where the self in all of its wonder and complexity, and what is real and true about identity, reside.

*   *   *

For Lisa Robertson, architectural spaces are artifacts of this struggle, that interplay of power between individual and collective, and all of the implicit constructions of race, class, gender, and sexuality that collectivity implies. Like Beer and Theis, she interrogates the interstitial spaces between self and performance, between speech and silence, between rooms within the same "spacio-economic system." As the satisfyingly dense essays in this volume unfold before us, Robertson posits architectural space as a voice in and of itself, the articulation of a shared cultural imagination, its valuations, and its hierarchies.

In many ways, this extended metaphor – of spatial design as collective voice, as articulation of power – comes through most visibly in Robertson's portrayal of archival spaces in "Doubt and the History of Scaffolding." She writes near the beginning of the essay,

> The history of scaffolding has been dismantled. We can't write this history because there are so few documents – only a slim sheaf of photographs. So we study the construction of the present and form theories. We use the alphabet as a ladder.

What is particularly revealing about this passage is the way that the objects furnishing a given room become an exercise in exclusion, become an erasure of voice and its once infinite possibilities. Here "the construction of the present," its visibility in the archive, offers a window into a culture's implicit judgments about history, and more specifically, what histories are worth preserving. Indeed, the exclusion of everything but "a slim sheaf of photographs" represents a silencing of not only a particular aesthetics, but a disavowal of the laboring class, its artisans, and their rich discursive history. Robertson reveals this absence as a subtle manifestation of power, a tacit affirmation of disenfranchisement and of hierarchy. In other words, it is a refusal to "to register, to list."

The book is perhaps most fascinating when Robertson engages the disparity between actual architectures and the aspirational discourses surrounding this discipline. Robertson explains that "[w]e believe that the object of architecture is to give happiness." By describing the pleasure given by inhabiting a particular space as "gift," suggesting care, forethought, and perhaps a bit of extravagance, is to call attention to the shortcomings of so many rooms, the impossibility of their aspirations, as they accumulate before us.

For Robertson, architecture is a voice marked only by its false promises, its silent wielding of power. It is a shifting power, one that metamorphoses as much as we do the moment we open the door, as soon as we cross the threshold into that darkening expanse. Like Beer and Theis, Robertson gives voice to our own desires within these spaces, as we long for a bit of music to ground us in the passage between anteroom and corridor, a greater "stability in the transitions between gestures."

"WHETHER IT'S COMING OR LEAVING WE CAN'T SAY": DESIRE & PROXIMITY IN THREE EXPERIMENTAL TEXTS

WALTER BENJAMIN ONCE NOTED THAT "the only way of knowing a person is to love them without hope." In other words, when we abandon intentionality it becomes possible to see again, to apprehend the other with clarity and compassion. To fully inhabit the present moment in such a way is to break temporarily from oneself, to lose sight of futurity and one's place within it. Yet it is far more commonplace to consider proximity in light of desire, to see a design in the narrative when all that is really there is "a girl," "a borrowed bicycle," a cache of "white petals absorbing ink."

Three recent experimental texts fully do justice to this complex relationship between proximity, wanting, and intention. Chloe Honum's *Then, Winter*, Anthony Varallo's *Everyone Was There*, and Kelly Magee's *The Neighborhood* each offer an incisive discussion of the infinite ways we are othered by our own desires, as it is our wishes that isolate us, hold us captive, blind us from the "fluorescent light" that is right there in the room with us. Though vastly different in style and approach, these three writers share an investment in exploring the infinite ways that sorrow and proximity, desire and otherness can exist in the same narrative space.

With that in mind, what is left unsaid is perhaps most telling in each of these collections. What the voice knows and cannot know about the other, what is known about the other and cannot be spoken, even to oneself, reveals far more about the narrator, her intentions, and her place in the story's graceful arc. Indeed, knowledge and proximity, distance and the imagination, become matters of choice. Throughout each collection, we are offered a beauty "so far away that it doesn't seem to exist," a loveliness at arm's reach that is not as gratifying or as true. For Varallo,

Honum and Magee, there is an abiding sense of closeness, but one that does not satisfy, a proximity that falls short. "If it would set me free, I would stay," Honum explains.

*   *   *

In Honum's *Then, Winter*, desire has distance built into its very making. As a result, proximity merely dulls the imagination, sets fire to the speaker's gorgeous fictive topographies. As Honum drifts between faultlessly constructed lines and pristine prose stanzas, we see that distance is that aperture that allows the mind, and its dreams, inside, a widening expanse that one may adorn with one's own shimmering narrative edifice. In many ways, this notion of distance as spark, distance as opportunity is enacted most visibly in the disconnect between interior and exterior, that which surrounds the speaker and her own psychic landscape.

Honum writes, for example, in "Late Afternoon in the Psychiatric Ward,"

> Now a fly throws itself
>
> down on the formica table
> and buzzes and spins
> on its back, quickening
>
> the poison. It resembles
> a word scribbled out.
> *Won't do, won't do.*
>
> But oh you of the river –
> wet lips, I miss you
> this moment, and this.

Here Honum calls our attention to the ways distance makes possible desire, as there is something inherently satisfying about incompleteness, which represents an invitation to imagine. In many ways, the poems' setting only heightens this tension between reality and the speaker's psychic landscapes, reminding us of not only their artifice, but also, their inherent unreliability. The collection is perhaps most striking when reality and an unstable imagination begin to merge, as we see in the transformation of the "fly," which becomes "a word scribbled out," metamorphosing again into a commentary on the narrative's trajectory: *"Won't do, won't do."*

Yet what is not spoken in Honum's collection is even more revealing. Because the reader is never once privy to a description of the love object, they too are implicated in this imaginative work. Just as Honum's cultivation of distance, and the impossibility of this desire, ignites her speaker's luminous dreaming, the reader, too, is prompted to participate in the fulfillment of desire through the creation of narrative. As Honum herself writes, "I take the rock, / I wish you were here, / and I pass the basket on."

*   *   *

Kelly Magee's *The Neighborhood* complicates this exploration of proximity, desire, and otherness. Throughout this collection of linked short stories, readers will encounter "mermaids washed ashore," a towering "pedestal," and a woman's body "found in a ravine." Though vastly different in their subject matter and implicit logic, the stories in this collection are gracefully unified by their consideration of the ways distance distorts one's thinking, allowing the object of perception to be othered by and through narrative.

Magee's abiding interest in the ways the imagination amplifies distance surfaces perhaps most visibly in the collection's opening story, "The Merm Prob." Indeed, Magee capitalizes on all that the reader has imagined about mermaids, as well as the mythology that our culture has built around this elusive, enigmatic figure. To say *mermaid* is to conjure a vast mythology of sirens, of song, of the feminine and its kinship with ephemerality and unattainability.

Instead of building on this imaginative work, Magee ingeniously chooses to show us the mythic mermaid at close proximity, close to the point of readerly discomfort:

> At the town meetings, we emphasized the merms' nature as wild things, more animal than human. Look at how they ate, for example, swallowing live fish whole. They could turn anything into a weapon, so we had to stop giving them utensils. A couple of us had wounds to prove it. *You don't know fear until you've had a fork flung at your kneck*, someone said, but we rolled our eyes at that. We knew fear.

She reminds us that it is distance that makes possible fiction, the narrative impulse arising from what we do not know, what we do not yet want to know. Indeed, she subtly and skillfully reveals the desire for distance as a wish for story, a graceful arc that ends abruptly when the object of attention is no longer held at some remove.

For Magee, this frightening closeness, this unwanted proximity, represents a kind of cruelty, an idea is implied by the muted violence and veiled threats that populate her stories. She elaborates in "The Pedestal," "The day she fell was a hard one. We'd let it go on too long, past the point we were comfortable with. One of us should have done it, we knew, brought her down and put her in a home." This slow and soundless distancing is revealed as not only a kind of violence, but an undoing, a removal of the love object from the world and its pleasures. As Magee herself notes, "The moral of the story is not what they thought it was."

*   *   *

Much like Magee's stories and Honum's poetry, Varallo's *Everyone Was There* considers distance as a kind of subtle violence, but one that we wish upon ourselves. This representation of proximity as a foreclosure of possibility, an end to the imagination, is enacted as much in the style of these carefully wrought stories as the content.

Presented as a series of flash fictions, which border at times on poetry, Vallaro's prose texts ultimately involve the reader in this othering of the love object through the creation of narrative. By holding the reader at some remove, revealing only enough to spark her imaginative work, Varallo proffers the text as the object of desire, the narrative in all of its richness as impossible union. Yet it is this distancing effect that calls out to the reader across the widening expanse, and entangles them further in the book's subtle and disconcerting imaginative topography.

In "Hunger," for example, Varallo writes,

> He had this way of eating them where he'd bite the cashew in half while holding the other half with his fingers, sniffing it, just for a second, on the sly. Then he'd eat the other half and repeat the whole thing again. We watched ballgames, sitcoms, evening news. But all I was thinking about were the cashews. Why had I turned them down? I wanted them more than anything.

Given the fact that the story ends there, the questions begin to multiply. Indeed, one might argue that the narrator's refusal of the cashews, which he "wanted...more than anything" was an effort to stave off something else entirely, perhaps a deeper kinship, camaraderie, or the possibility of becoming the other as a result of this unwanted closeness, to find himself unwittingly "eating" and "sniffing" in such an odd, ritualistic manner. As the book unfolds, kind of generative ending becomes a trope, meaning, in this case, a unifying aspect of the writer's voice and style. Each story, each discrete episode ultimately refines an already subtle power dynamic between text and reader. By withholding meaning, Varallo inevitably retains the upper hand, keeping the reader in a state of speculation, of hopeful anticipation. As a result, the book becomes a machine for generating meaning, and when its wheels turn, one cannot help but look.

*   *   *

If one must abandon intention in order to truly know, what is possible beyond the boundaries of formal knowledge?

For Magee, Varallo, and Honum, knowing is a choice, a decision to relinquish the imagination, to abandon the mind's luminous dreamscapes, for more stable ground. Though vastly different in style and approach, their collections offer a similarly incisive exploration of the danger inherent in this certainty. To understand is to live without possibility, to dream only of what has already come to pass. In writing that is powerful in both its narrative and its silences, these gifted writers show us, fearlessly and provocatively, that knowing is only beautiful insofar as it allows us to dream.

LYRIC ADDRESS:
IMPOSSIBLE DESIRE, INFINITE POSSIBILITY

EMANUEL LEVINAS ONCE ARGUED that intimacy takes us from the impossible, to the infinite, and back again. In this interstitial space, we are transfixed by the boundlessness of another consciousness—a luminous, intricate, self-contained world that is ultimately inaccessible. Yet this vastness continues to reveal itself, offering glimpses of a psychic terrain that lies just beyond what one can know.

Three recent collections of poetry offer constructions of intimacy that fully and convincingly acknowledge this complexity: Jennifer S. Cheng's *House A*, Rochelle Hurt's *In Which I Play the Runaway*, and Karen Volkman's *Whereso*. Through their novel and provocative variations on traditional lyric address, these poets reveal closeness as a kind of "corporeal speech" that forever equivocates. In each collection, we are asked to consider, albeit through a slightly different conceptual lens, our eternal alterity, that all-too-familiar condition of "wanting the world through a window," as Hurt describes it.

With that in mind, the presentation of the "you" is perhaps most telling in these finely crafted book-length sequences. The love object is both a "cross-section of water," impossible to render, and a gravitational pull. We are made to see the allure (and the impossibility) of a sustained, meaningful moment of recognition, that "faraway hour" when both the "I" and the "you" fully reveal themselves to one another. Each poem, and the silences that accompany them, remind us that someone else's mind is like an ocean, "fluid and wafting in refracted light." What's more, these gifted and dexterous poets know that despite this persistent "unmooring," this "willful" and "soundless" distancing, "the body will blur its boundary, will embrace."

*   *   *

Cheng observes, in a recent craft essay published in *The Black Warrior Review*, that every story of intimacy is haunted by "a shadow story." For Cheng, this hidden narrative is almost always the history of language itself. *House A*, her first full-length collection of poems, shows us the "chaos and wholeness" of a voice that is sedimented with its own past, even in the most personal moments of lyric address. Indeed, the speaker's lexicon is revealed as being at once mediated and insular, a social construct that ultimately isolates. "We each live within our own language," Cheng explains, and any closeness, any true connection requires "stitching these languages together." Yet speech is not as simple as the relationship between signifier and signified. Rather, Cheng reminds us that the larger structures of power and authority that surround us are embedded, and enacted, within our smallest grammatical choices. "And how relieved I was," she writes, "no longer to be embarrassed by my mother's voice but to feel her broken sounds again as intimacy, as home." Here, we are othered by and through language, as each inflection, each "folktale" slowly reveals an "anchoring of place." After all, it is an individual's movement through language that allows us to situate them amidst the inevitably contested borders and territories that make up a larger body politic. Language, for Cheng, is an "*inhabited surface*, like the wooden grain surrounding an embedded nail."

It is perhaps for these reasons that Cheng's book begins by depicting an impossible intimacy. Presented as an epistolary exchange, "Letters to Mao" allows us to witness the "man of history we know so well" being presented with the speaker's most private familial exchanges. In much the same way that language (and its political implications) infiltrate the farthest corners of the mind, Mao is shown the "the dark silhouette of a mother's hair," "the dust and corners" of a home. Any intimacy is revealed as both deeply personal and inevitably collective, as it is mediated by a shared historical imagination.

Indeed, the closeness that Cheng's speaker cultivates—whether through lyric address, memory, or the creation of narrative—is persistently intruded upon. As the sequence unfolds, a "mother's off-key lullabies" and even "the movement of a body in sleep" become an "island that wasn't even yours." Cheng writes, for instance,

> Dear Mao,
> I want to describe for you the watery life of home, and by that I do not mean the ambiguity of homeland. For homeland is something embalmed in someone else's memory, or it is a symbol, both close to the heart and a stranger you reach for in the middle of the night...

Here the lyric becomes a performance of what has been lost, becomes elegy, and finally, becomes an impossibility. By entering language, we have surrendered an essential part of ourselves, and as a result, we have given over our ability to share that "small" and "tunneling" space with another. Yet Cheng upholds the possibility of compassion and connection, even in a divisive, sometimes hostile cultural landscape. Although the speaker's "homeland" is described as an "ambiguity," and the recipient of this deeply personal letter is a mere "symbol," both are still held "close to the heart." Fittingly, the voice of empire never speaks back, but rather, becomes a conduit for "the biography of the collective," a "spreading of constellations across a dark chart."

*   *   *

Rochelle Hurt's first collection, *The Rusted City*, is marked by a decidedly polyphonic approach to both narrative and the lyric. Reminiscent of Virginia Woolf's *The Waves*, Hurt shows us that the creation of any story is a shared endeavor, as each "wife," each "quiet mother" takes turns describing the "impatient decay" that surrounds her. Hurt's latest book, *In Which I Play the Runaway*, returns to this enduring interest in collective consciousness, while also bringing her multi-voiced lyricism to bear on concerns that only occupied the periphery of her earlier work.

Hurt's second collection, much like Cheng's *House A*, considers the ways intimacy is mediated by a shared cultural imagination. A fugitive speaker drifts between personae and voices, among them "Aunt Em," "Dorothy," and "The Lone Ranger." In this intricately crafted sequence, any semblance of empathy, love, or understanding is buried, "splintered with shreds / of unfamiliar syllables," beneath a heaping accumulation of received narratives.

"The sky behind you," she writes, "is a sherbet pastiche of movie set hues." Here the narratives that connect us, making possible shared experience and culture, are also an intrusion into the most intimate parts of the psyche. Hurt shows us, skillfully and strikingly, that the stories and archetypes which provide frameworks for our thinking, that build community across geographic and temporal boundaries, are also a subtle and deeply unsettling presence in what we once thought were private exchanges. As "silence blooms" between the speaker of these gorgeous poems and her absent beloved(s), we see her unmoored by the very characters she aspires to, who ultimately keep her "houseless" and "husbandless."

Like Cheng, she shows us the lyric "I" as inevitably collective, undoubtedly mediated. What distinguishes Hurt's collection, however, is her unflinching presentation of her speaker's "breaking" and "slippery" psyche. Because of this proliferation of narrative—that "empty grave" of postmodern culture—the "I" is persistently drifting, ambulatory. "I fall in love with surfaces," Hurt writes. She elucidates for us, bravely and strikingly, that the depth of emotion, the "honeymoon" to which every film and novel aspires, has become an impossibility, an indistinct and beautiful memory, "a perpetual past tense" that haunts the luminous, vast, "brimming" mass media circulating around us.

*　　　*　　　*

Much like Volkman's previous collections, *Whereso* situates the individual voice within a linguistic landscape that is temporally bound and sedimented with history. We are made to see, whether in the Petrarchan sonnets of *Nomina*, or hybrid prose of *Spar*, the ways that received forms of discourse structure our most private interactions. Yet *Whereso* also explores the agency of the individual in language, the myriad ways that "the throat-flute uttering its constant note" offers a kind of subtle resistance.

For Volkman, it is the intrusion of language, this ever-present strangeness within the self, that makes intimacy possible. Like Cheng and Hurt, she fully acknowledges the ways that the mind is mediated by grammar and culture. Yet she shows us, deftly and compellingly, that these received narratives can be fractured, "collapsed into particles," remade entirely. It is through this cracked lens, this "totality of pieces," that we come to know and truly understand the other. For Volkman, the inevitable "levitation into clarity" cannot be anything other than mediated, as it is this commonality, this "bridge," that "makes the force containable," that gives us language and structure for our experiences.

In this collection of intricately linked poems, Volkman offers a lyric "I" that is at once fragmented and charged with desire. "A contour of relation," she writes, "swells, hurls." It is no coincidence that many of these poems take place in the old world, replete with "pageant," inhabited by a speaker who "loves" these monuments and ruins "as material." Here, intimacy is none other than an encounter with cultural memory, "needle-bright and bleeding," as it is made and unmade by another consciousness. This unequivocal embrace of intimacy as mediation—and desire as only possible because it is bounded by time and history—most distinguishes Volkman's poems from those of Cheng and Hurt.

As *Whereso* unfolds, this "retrouvé of the past-pulse" is enacted in the very texture of the language itself, offering a vision of the lyric that is as polyphonic and historically sedimented as it is electric.

She writes in "Stranger Report,"

> no gesture
> can arrest
> crawling or leaping
> both are a deeping
>
> of traceable action, intentions on a stage. We are
> your auditors, calculating ruptures, in the invisible
> lines determining
>
> movement as pattern, this precision beyond a norm.

Here the lyric "I" arises from a confluence of vastly different lexicons and registers. The language of business ("traceable action," "we are your auditors") collides beautifully and seamlessly with academic diction ("calculating rupture") and everyday speech ("this precision beyond a norm"). Volkman asks us to consider, through her careful juxtapositions, voice as a social construct, all of thought as a collective endeavor, even when one believes one is alone. *Whereso* is filled with gorgeous poems like this one, which show us, strikingly and effortlessly, that it is "the textures and tinctures" of received culture that allow us to truly appreciate the other, because they prompt us to speak and—finally, inevitably— be understood.

*   *   *

If intimacy is both an impossible desire and infinite possibility, lyric address may very well be an attempt to think through this contradiction. In these three striking volumes of poetry, one encounters this paradox in all of its beauty and complexity. Here, we are offered a carefully constructed philosophy of interpersonal connection, which is at once boundless and bound by the realities of human consciousness.

What's more, it is through their innovative constructions of poetic voice, their polyphonic and formally dexterous approach to the lyric, that we begin to recognize the constant presence of the other within the self. Whether offering a lyric "I" that is multi-voiced or a "you" who exists as inaccessible radiance, these poets show us intimacy as mediated, and mediation as a kind of intimacy in itself. We are never alone with the other, because we are never alone with ourselves.

THE MIND SET ALIGHT: SUZANNE BUFFAM'S A PILLOW BOOK & KATHRYN NUERNBERGER'S BRIEF INTERVIEWS WITH THE ROMANTIC PAST

THE EXISTENTIAL PHILOSPHERS DESCRIBED LIGHT as "awakened consciousness," the mind made real by an entire world bearing down on the senses. Perception is more than the simple act of apprehending; memory comes to us first through the body, as does grief, and wishing, and terror. With that in mind, the unfolding of conscious experience is inevitably an embodied endeavor, as much as perception is bounded by time, narrative, and history.

Two recent collections of lyric prose offer representations of consciousness, history, and the body that do justice to this complexity. Suzanne Buffam's *A Pillow Book* and Kathryn Nuernberger's *Brief Interviews with The Romantic Past* trace the lovely arc of the mind through "the Siege of Paris," a woman's sleepless year, and dimly lit rooms "at the turn of the tenth century." By moving through time in a nonlinear way, Buffam and Nuernberger show us that there is never a perception "happened across in the dark;" rather, to apprehend the world is to be inundated with its discontents and the various narratives of history and difference to which they give rise.

Though somewhat divergent in style and approach, Nuernberger and Buffam share an investment in revealing thought as not only embodied, but also inherently relational. In these skillfully constructed collections of lyric prose, the boundary between self and world falls away; "wing-beating swans" spark the inner life of Nuernberger's lively narrator, and likewise, the presence of the protagonist's husband, "picking nettles in the graveyard," alters the trajectory of the mind, even in what may appear to be her most isolated moments.

*   *   *

In *Brief Interviews with the Romantic Past*, the senses are a source of constant transformation. "Her white dress of a body cleaves the foreground of flames," Nuernberger writes. Here, and elsewhere in the book, one's physical being is a catalyst for metaphor, the imagination, and its lavish topographies. In much the same way that Madame Blanchard's "white dress of a body" quickly becomes image and emblem, the "youngest brother" is descried as having to "live with a single wing dangling off his body like a form of amputation or miracle." We find ourselves increasingly– and purposefully–unsure where the body ends and myth begins. Nuernberger, subtly and skillfully, presents a vision of physicality and the senses as mediated by the various narratives that circulate within culture. Within the imagined landscape of this collection, these mediating forces range from prevailing ideas about femininity (and the difficult loveliness inherent in "little jewelry box of a life she had"), to aesthetics (for example, the "strange and unexpected beauty of sound"), and science ("…the corpse of a hanged man has been laid out on the table and the gallery teems with men trying to understand what it means to be alive…."). One's experience of any "pretty thing, fluttering over the flowers" is never truly one's own, but rather, it is always informed by one's place in a larger cultural landscape.

In these gorgeously rendered essays, we find a narrator who inevitably, and candidly, allows "the mind to inflict its impressions on the body." Her "hands" and "milky face" becomes ledger, repository for narratives that are rarely–if ever–her own. Nuernberger writes, for instance, in "Why the Dauphin Won't Consummate the Marriage,"

> The gates at Versailles had been left open for so many years, they could not be shut against the mob because of rust. Any man with a sword at his side was welcome to walk through the palace. Any woman with a proper dress could come to watch her queen eat. It was the duty of the royal family to let their

people see them live.

What's perhaps most telling about this passage is the way Nuernberger situates the body – and its accompanying perceptions – within a larger narrative of nationhood. For the queen, to "live" in one's own skin, to move through the various rooms of the palace, is also to function as symbol, as archetype. Every "woman in a proper dress" who arrives as spectator, every "man with a sword at his side" who traipses through "the gates at Versailles" serves as a reminder of the mythologies that make her, for which the queen is only a conduit. As she sits down to "eat," and as she prepares each morning "to live," she is never alone with her senses because she is never alone with herself. Here Nuernberger reminds us, with subtlety and grace, of the constant presence of the other within the self, that "slowly burning" light that allows us to see where one's fingertips end and "the wind-whipped night sky" begins.

* * *

Much like Nuernberger's *Brief Interviews with the Romantic Past*, Suzanne Buffam's gorgeous hybrid text interrogates the boundaries between self and world. *Yet A Pillow Book* also prompts us to consider the implications when self *becomes* world, the subject having taken the detritus of culture – its "exhaustive catalogues of petty grievances," its ongoing "blather" – to create an insular, entirely self-contained psychic landscape.

Presented in a series of discrete prose meditations, which take the form of lists, histories, and micro-narratives, the luminous fragments in Buffam's collection orbit gracefully around the recurring theme of sleeplessness. In many ways, she proffers the text as a metaphor for the narrator's "restless" and "oversensitive" mind, its surface a ledger onto which the narratives of twenty-first century culture have been written, erased, and revised. Indeed, *A Pillow Book* retains a palimpsestic quality, as the symbols, myths, and images that populate shared culture are appropriated and transformed:

I and It, by Martin Buber.
Queen Lear, by William Shakespeare.
Moby Dick, by Gertrude Stein.
End Game, by Dr. Seuss.
Complete Poems, by Sappho.

Here literary history is reimagined as metaphor, made to enact what is purely an interior drama. The common language of culture is rendered suddenly unrecognizable, as it is fashioned in the likeness of the individual psyche, made to reflect its entirely singular preoccupations. While it is impossible to occupy only "the gauzy white stuff of dreams," Buffam shows a psyche that has willfully, recklessly, distanced itself from the conversation that sustains it. Yet it is a disturbance of the body's equilibrium that ultimately unhinges the narrator's mind. Every fragment of the larger world, and their accompanying narratives, are brought to bear on the ache of a body is persistently, relentlessly "unwell."

For instance, Buffam writes,

> Among the Ngoni of modern Tanzania, the feather-stuffed pillow is considered so intimate a possession it is often buried with its owner. When a chief among the Shona of modern South Africa dies, his pillow is passed on to his successor, who prays to it, as to the spirit of his ancestor, in times of crisis before sleep. Among the Luba of the Democratic Republic of the Congo, when the body of the deceased is unavailable for burial, as is often the case given present political realities, his or her pillow is buried instead.

Here the nerve-wracked physical body is revealed as both a confinement and a beautiful escape. Indeed, Buffam posits sleep as a domain unto itself, much like the underworld of ancient mythologies. Yet she also portrays this imaginative topography as incredibly "intimate," specific and tailored to – no, arising from - that individual's psyche. Although the "successor" prays to his "feather stuffed pillow" before "a time of crisis," Buffam shows us that the true catastrophe is not the political, but rather, it is existential. Sleep itself is revealed as a "burial," as the protagonist retreats deeper and deeper into her own subjectivity.

*   *   *

If the mind is made real only by the world's intrusions, then perhaps narrative is one's an attempt to document that process of becoming.

Certainly, Buffam's *A Pillow Book* and Nuernberger's *Brief Interviews with the Romantic Past* offer vastly different ways of conceptualizing the relationship between perception, consciousness, and the lovely arc of story. Yet the two collections raise similar questions about the possibility – or impossibility – of an unmediated experience of the world around us. For both Buffam and Nuernberger, the presence of a shared imagination, this collective consciousness, helps us find order and structure for the unbounded chaos of perception. What's more, these gifted and dexterous writers remind us that once the "daylight" and "the sparkle and splash" of water have been apprehended, it is the presence of this common language that allows to us – finally, and inevitably – to speak.

BEAUTY, RISK, & THE PARATEXT:
ON RECENT WORK BY SARAH ANN WINN, CARRIE LORIG, & SARAH MINOR

IN A RECENT *NEW YORK TIMES* ARTICLE on the history of artistic innovation, Costica Bradatan states unequivocally that "change comes from the margins." Indeed, he cites the work of Tzara, Loy, and other Dadaist practitioners, who frequently flaunted their otherness as though it were a badge of honor, or further evidence of their progressive thinking. Yet Bradatan's argument could be taken much more literally, as a testament to the endless possibility inherent in a number of distinct paratextual zones.

We tend to forget that any prose text is governed by a clear set of hierarchies, which enact judgments about the relative importance of various types of language and modes of thinking. The text proper is reserved for what is truly illuminating, with footnotes, glossaries, appendices and endnotes being tertiary, orbiting around this supposedly radiant center. Yet because the main text is burdened by the weight of knowing, the margins are rife with possibility, and bursting with light. Recent years have seen a proliferation of experimental works, which utilize the techniques of both conceptual poetry and scholarly prose. Taking the form of mislaid glossaries, unruly footnotes, and wildly imaginative annotations, these hybrid texts—Jenny Boully's *The Body: An Essay*, Kristy Bowen's *In the Bird Museum*, and Kim Gek Lin Short's *The Bugging Watch* being merely a few examples—remind us that the margins are more conducive to risk, and more amenable to moments of beauty and wonder, than a main text constrained by its own importance, and halted by a burden of readerly expectation.

Sarah Ann Winn's *Field Guide to Alma Avenue and Frew Drive*, Carrie

Lorig's *The Book of Repulsive Women*, and Sarah Minor's *The Persistence of the Bonyleg: Annotated* continue this necessary exploration of the freedom inherent in the paratext. Although vastly different in style and approach, these exquisite collections share an investment of questioning the hierarchies that tend to impose upon the various components of a prose work. Here we are made to experience the sorrow of inhabiting a main text "littered with all the wrong words," glowing with an "unfamiliar light." What's more, we encounter the "oblong memory of loss," a "sudden gulp of regret" as they sprawl beyond the boundaries of traditional narrative, as annotations and spare, singing fragments become the text proper. In each of these stunning volumes, we are reminded of what possibility lies beneath buried underneath a conventional prose paragraph, that "still body of water," that "lake too large to shout across."

*   *   *

In Winn's *Field Guide to Alma Avenue and Frew Drive*, the margins offer a point of entry to a stunning exploration of the lyric fragment, its unique artistic possibilities, and its inherent limitations. Taking the form of seemingly endless appendices, which remain unattached to a main text, the poems in this carefully curated collection remind us that the paratext is not fraught with the pressures of wholeness or cohesion. Indeed, Winn turns to the margins because they are more amenable to fragments of "old paper," the "dog-eared pages crisp for her tongue."

As the book unfolds, we are made to see there is a certain line of thinking that is only possible within fractured language, as more traditional forms often foreclose the wild associative leaps and ruptures that populate Winn's gorgeous, singing work. She writes, for example, in "Notes From In-House Field Survey,"

    + elders may be present singly or in pairs, always

accompanied by a child to study the lay of the land
in secret

+ recrumpled paper to reshape waves
+ calculated the number of pedal pushes past the
distant shore, graphed the lily pads, marked points
from the bottom of the low hill to the screen door
and then calculated the increase of stories in relation
to time

+ furtive ethnographer

It is in the space between "secrets" and "recrumpled paper" that
transformation becomes possible. As the first prose stanza unfolds,
we are presented with uncertainty after uncertainty: elders arrive
"singly or in pairs," a "child" shrouded in "secrecy' from a threat
that is never fully revealed to us. Each hypothesis, each conjecture
is described in a voice that is fully convincing in its stately tone, the
faultless logic of syntax, the implied causations of its grammatical
workings.   Upon transitioning to the second prose stanza,
however, one discovers that Winn's rhetorical mode has shifted
in the space between paratextual zones.   Indeed, we encounter a
voice that reflects on its making, a luminous and fierce machinery
that examines its own workings.   Indeed, the 'recrumpled paper"
and "reshaped waves" may be read as metaphors for the movement
of the text itself, which eventually becomes "a distant shore," the
reader a "furtive ethnographer," attempting to map a terrain that is
forever shifting.   In many ways, this is what makes Winn's work so
compelling, so gratifyingly subversive. The fractured form she has
chosen – appendices to appendices to a text that we cannot, and
may never, have access to – effectually evades the expectation, and
the strictures, of wholeness. In each gap, and within each moment
of rupture, we find the rules of the game have been wholly revised.
The paratext, with its fissures and elisions, is filled with liminal
spaces, in which nearly anything becomes possible.

*   *   *

Much like Winn's collection, Lorig's *The Book of Repulsive Women* envisions the paratext as a space for transformation. Here, though, paratext becomes palimpsest, as both the main text and its proliferations are erased and written over again and again. Presented as several possible or alternate versions of the same piece, Lorig's work also positions itself in relation to John Berryman's *The Dream Songs*, as the phrase "John Berryman's Feminist Revenge" is repeated and in this repetition, is transfigured. Yet the work reads more as revision of Berryman's text than annotation. It is "an essay on distance and estrangement," as exegesis becomes a space for interrogation, irreverence, and eventually reversals of power. In many ways, the work's orientation as paratext makes possible this questioning, this *coup d'etat*, as one finds greater motive for revolution when placed firmly in the margins.

Lorig reminds us, as Jenny Boully did in her seminal work, *The Body: An Essay*, that women's voices have, in essence been confined to these paratextual zones. Yet Lorig reimagines what is possible within this rhetorical space. Indeed, the margins are no longer exclusively for "citation," but rather, they become an "intervention" that is rife with possibility. Lorig writes, for instance, midway through the collection:

> The Narrative Mouth—
> Lilacs—
> Cézanne—
>
> > Nobody else
> > Nobody else but yours Nobody else but
> > These This
> > They can't copy it.

Lorig gestures at both the predominantly male artistic tradition she has inherited and the accompanying expectations of the female voice, which frequently involve "lilacs" and the ever-present conventions of "narrative." Lorig shows us that "the narrative mouth" that speaks in much of literature is also heteronormative in its assumptions, as the speaker recounts the readerly expectations, values, and judgments that are inevitably internalized: "Nobody else / Nobody else but yours…" Yet as the book unfolds, each incarnation of *The Book of Repulsive Women*, and each iteration of the speaker's voice, grows more unruly. Indeed, we encounter "blood and rags," the female spectator turned voyeur ("…she filmed them…"). The marginal space is revealed as sublimated violence, as repression turned outward. "There is a devil inside me / there is a flower inside me," Lorig writes. We understand, suddenly, and irrevocably, how both can be true at once.

*   *   *

Minor's *The Persistence of Bonyleg: Annotated*, like the work of Winn and Lorig, re-envisions what is possible in the margins of a prose text. Here, though, main text and paratext are coeval, emerging at the same moment, as part of the same imaginative topography. What's more, they fuel one another, intertwining like a "coniferous forest," that place "where spruce spines string Europe to China and Mongolia to the arctic arc." As the sequence progresses, and as we find ourselves more and more lost in its luminous "folds" of "ribbon," Minor subtly challenges many of our preconceived notions about the paratext, particularly the idea that text and paratext are separate entities, with different intentions and divergent motives. Minor certainly questions the hierarchies that are often imposed upon the various components of a prose work, but also, she interrogates our notions of textual ownership inherent in this division, showing us that all of language is a collective endeavor, a conversation, a confluence.

In many ways, Minor's investment in language as collectively voiced, as a social endeavor is most visible in the evolution of the "narrator." Appearing first as a kind of lyrical voiceover, responding to and clarifying a main text in which "the Lykovs were a family of six Old Believers who followed a river…into the wilderness," the narrator's sections become increasingly dialogic, more and more dependent upon other voices, other texts, and other textures of language as the work unfolds. Minor elaborates,

> 1. **Scientists:** "At first we had a hard time understanding the daughters' speech. Their way of speaking was unique—a muffled, nasal chanting. When the sisters talked to each other, it sounded like a slow, blurred cooing."

> 2. **Narrator:** This I is shifting, okay? Over there, I was a schismatic. I's own birth was an act of rebellion.

> 3. **Fairytale:** The taiga is a swath of coniferous forest—the world's largest Terrestrial Biome. Eleven percent of the northern hemisphere. You go in by helicopter….

Here, and throughout the collection, Minor has created a voice that reflects on its own movement through an inherently unstable cultural landscape. Indeed, the "I" is perpetually "shifting," its "birth" an "act of rebellion" against the all too static categories of language, genres, and texts.

What's more, Minor's enduring interest in all of speech as collective, and voice as a social construct, is enacted in the style of the writing itself. The narrator is eventually revealed as the "daughter" subjected to the scrutiny of the scientists, those purveyors of reason who "had a hard time understanding" her "speech." As we transition from speaker to speaker, we find that every texture of language, and each discourse that Minor inhabits, culls material from the others. Indeed, the scientifically minded rhetoric at the very beginning of the quoted passage proves necessary when describing the fairy tale's "taiga," posited as "the world's largest Terrestrial Biome," comprising "eleven percent of the northern hemisphere." In much the same way that Minor's "I" "was a "schismatic," we discover that these disparate, often divergent voices constitute what is in essence a dialogue between part of the self, or parts of consciousness. Approached with that in mind, text and paratext are revealed not as separate things, under "confinement," but instead parts of "a collective work," "a mirror."

THEATER OF THE MIND: ON RECENT PERFORMANCE TEXTS BY KHADIJAH QUEEN & MEREDITH STRICKER

IN THE *UNAVOWABLE COMMUNITY*, MAURICE BLANCHOT considers the impossibility of fully apprehending another consciousness. If the other could be known, he argues, they would not be other. We are confronted with that which resists one's powers of understanding, a strangeness that becomes the source of great and terrible wonder. Yet this line of thinking could also be extended to the various parts of the self, none of which can ever be fully or satisfyingly excavated. What's more, these darkened rooms of the mind are furnished with artifacts that the other has left behind: a forgotten trinket, an old book, a bit of music.

Two recent performance texts consider the many ways that the other is contained within the self. Khadijah Queen's *Non-Sequitur* and Meredith Stricker's *Alphabet Theater* skillfully dramatize this ongoing dialogue between the various parts of consciousness, giving voice to the alterity that is contained within each one of us. Though vastly different in form and approach, Stricker and Queen share an investment in revealing consciousness itself as performative, as one assumes (and at the same time questions) the roles of the various archetypes, their voices, their personae, and their possibilities. We are presented with a consciousness that is divided, not always against itself, but in dialogue with its seemingly infinite and luminous facets. As each work progresses, we are made to see how conscious experience unfolds through this questioning, this conversation and exchange.

Though these performance texts might be read as purely interior dramas, we are shown that the world is contained within each of us. Indeed, Queen and Stricker envision the mind as comprised almost entirely of found material, ranging from Hart Crane's *The Bridge* to "the voice of Malcolm X." Through their skillful curation of language, Queen and Stricker reveal the mind as a social construct, thought as appropriation, and every idea as an act of theft.

*   *   *

Queen's provocative *Non-Sequitur* takes place everywhere and nowhere. We are offered a cast consisting of archetypes, what Queen describes as a "large group of abstract/conceptual characters and objects," none of which give rise to a conventional narrative. Instead, Queen delivers "a shifting landscape" and "evolving interiors," each conversation taking the form of an excavation of culture and the psyche. Every act, and every scene, contained within *Non-Sequitur* confronts a source tension that heretofore has remained buried, an unacknowledged violence that we soon find "engulfed in a spotlight."

Many of the vignettes presented within *Non-Sequitur* consider the ways race and gender are performative, how these concepts of identity exist in dialogue and in friction with one another. Indeed, Queen calls our attention to the myriad ways that the "invisible institution" with its constant demands, "the white appropriation," the looming "online payments" and the systems of valuation that they represent, are inevitably internalized. What Queen offers us is an externalization of the conceptual frameworks we have taken in; it is this visible and visceral rendering that allows us to see their reach more clearly, to understand that we are not only subjected to injustice, but it is an "aftermath" we carry inside of us.

Queen writes, for example, midway through the collection,

> THE INVISIBLE INSTITUTION
> Playing with children, playing with adults –
> same thing.

> THE BROWN VAGINA (points to a door)
> Someone left the door open –

THE ONLINE PAYMENTS
Reminder: Please send payment by the due date.

Here Queen portrays the competing systems of valuation that one must constantly reconcile in the mind: the economies of labor, texts, and goods that circulate round us, as well as their relationship to the physical body, particularly the ways difference is written onto the body. By giving voice to each iniquity, and each projection, Queen reveals the impossibility of a harmonious and unified psyche. She suggests, skillfully and powerfully, that we have not only divided communities against themselves, but we have divided our own hearts and minds. As Queen accounts for each fissure, each cleave mark, she reminds us that even "intelligence is a kind of violence."

*   *   *

Stricker's *Alphabet Theater*, much like Queen's work, considers the way that conscious experience is an essentially social endeavor. She shows us that "even in dead winter" the "immense bee hum" of a larger cultural imagination is audible. Culling language from a variety of lexicons, which include Senator Danforth's speeches, the poetry of William Carlos Williams, and Milton's *Paradise Lost*, Stricker constructs a theory of mind in which we are constantly reconciling the texts, images, and symbols that circulate around us. For Stricker, it is in the space between these received texts, in these luminous apertures, that the individual begins to exist. As Stricker herself reminds us, "The more a thing is torn, the more places it can connect."

As the book unfolds, she reminds us thought is not as simple as "roses calling roses to mind." Indeed, she catalogues the seemingly infinite forms an inner life can take, allowing the various modes of knowledge and perception—which range from lists, to dialogues, staging directions, performance scripts, micronarratives, imaginary etymologies, and photographs—to illuminate one another. As the reader traipses through this "still place," filled with the luminous artifacts of an inner life, we find ourselves implicated in the process of forging connections, narratives, continuities. By involving the reader in such a way, Stricker shows us that to exist in culture is to enter a room filled with someone else's belongings; we are always strangers in our own psyches.

Stricker writes, for instance,

> the veins radiant in Thoreau's leaf
> or life – gladly, willingly –
> desire of the world for form, arc to arc – bright white
> we suffer from this bridge of lightening to loss

Stricker, like Queen, skillfully externalizes the conceptual frameworks—particularly the structures of meaning making, and the finite conventions of narrative —that we have taken in. By creating this distance, Stricker is able to discern more clearly implicit assumptions contained in the "forms" we search for. She calls our attention to the ways culture has taught us to impose structure, to create the loveliest "arc" we can from the materials we are given. It is this distance, the space between Stricker and her subject, that allows her to reveal our predilection for meaning in all of its beautiful artifice.

Queen and Stricker, while differing slightly in form and approach, both render the inner life suddenly, startlingly tangible, dramatizing the movement of conscious experience. In doing so, they allow us to perceive the mind, its "shining" fissures and its "islands" in sharper relief. Even more importantly, these innovative poets make solitude beautiful and strange again.

MELANCHOLY, WONDER & THE ARCHIVE
IN THREE RECENT POETRY COLLECTIONS

WALTER BENJAMIN ONCE DESCRIBED MEMORY as "the medium of past experience, just as the earth is the medium in which dead cities lie buried." Our recollection of events, then, is inevitably curated and constructed, in much the same way that "dead cities" are later mined, mapped, catalogued. The work of representation—of accounting for one's movement through time—often takes the form of such an excavation, in which we bring to light all that has been obscured by time's slow and soundless distancing.

Three recent collections of poetry engage archival material—whether personal or more broadly cultural—in ways that acknowledge and fully engage this complexity. In Joshua Beckman's *Shake*, Caroline Knox's *To Drink Boiled Snow*, and Lisa Olstein's *The Resemblance of the Enzymes of Grasses to Those of Whales Is a Family Resemblance*, we encounter language that is historically sedimented, reminding us of its own presence as an artistic "medium," one that is charged with subjectivity and doubt. Here the all-too-familiar impulse to create meaning is revealed as a kind of burial, in which past experience becomes "part of a world no one believes in." We are asked to consider—albeit from three vastly different conceptual vantage points—the distancing effects of language and narrative, the undoubtedly familiar experience of "shielding the eyes" while also "clouding the vision."

With that in mind, the construction of the speaker's voice is perhaps most telling in each of these finely crafted collections. We encounter a narrator who is stricken with awe while also mourning a world that is already past as soon as it is present. As each book unfolds, we are presented with "days" as they are "parsed with fine-toothed combs." What's more, we are made to see the allure (and difficulty) of closing the gap between ourselves and a shimmering past through our use of language. Each poem, and the ruptures that accompany them, remind us that rhetoric inevitably fails to bear us back from a luminous present. Indeed, the skillful shifts in voice and register enact the impossibility of that "little illusion," of "remembering how to return."

*   *   *

In Knox's *To Drink Boiled Snow*, one finds it difficult to situate the work's language in time. "A flange of ivy absorbed us," Knox writes, "I think this was vicarious Stamford, pale buildings oblique to the train." Here, and throughout the collection, arcane words—"flange," "oblique," etc.—are imbued with a startling immediacy. In many ways, this effect may be attributed to Knox's skillful manipulation of tone, as we are presented with a first-person speaker who speaks with both authority and urgency. "To skate on black ice is hard science," Knox insists. As the collection unfolds, we watch as language—in all of its formality and historicity—is borne into a luminous present through the poet's careful construction of voice.

Knox's poems also gesture at the impossibility of language existing outside of time. Though voiced with urgency, even outrage, the work is filled with provocative tension, especially when considering the interplay of tone and diction. Indeed, Knox's language often resists its placement in time. "I am Lark Crowe / You're Jay Wren / I guess we're a rebus," she explains. Here the formality of the word "rebus" strikes sparks against the more colloquial phrases in these lines (for example, "I guess"). Yet much of the work's meaning resides in these moments of rupture and disconnect, as though each poem was "lit from within." For instance, Knox writes,

> I gave my love a copy
> of *The Education of Henry Adams*
> He gave me a subscription
> to *The Journal of Fonzarelli Studies*

We went beside the river
in the snow sleet snow

Here Knox's use of outmoded words and phrases (for example: "my love") becomes a source of not only tension, but also, humor. When considering the overtly formal diction of these lines, which is amplified by the work's parallel syntactic constructions, the objects that populate this piece—particularly the "copy / of *The Education of Henry Adams*"—read almost as a commentary on the style of the writing. The speaker searches the archive for a proper vehicle for her affect, only to find "a copy" of someone else's biography, and "a subscription to *The Journal of Fonzarelli Studies*," neither of which functions as an appropriate signifier. As Knox delves deeper into the detritus of history and culture, the distance between signifier and signified seems only to become more palpable, suggesting the existence of language as barrier, as a widening expanse between ourselves and the "ruins" we seem to remember so clearly.

*   *   *

Beckman's *Shake*, much like Knox's *To Drink Boiled Snow*, explores the relationship between language and time. For Beckman, too, the language of the present moment falls short of fully conveying the speaker's affect, prompting him to mine the archive for a representation that seems more real and more true. "The thirst of the crowd. We laid the surfer down. / The child and the child," Beckman writes, "Come look what I have found." As in Knox's work, the archive emerges as a rhetorical space marked by its formality and aesthetic distance. The stately and regal tone of these lines, established by the declarative, almost biblical syntactic constructions, is amplified by the simplicity of the poet's diction. Here, and throughout the collection, Beckman places language that bisects time, possibly belonging to many different temporal moments (for instance "the child," "the thirst of the crowd," etc.) alongside phrases that are historically situated (i.e., "the surfer"). As a result, we are prompted to consider the inadequacy of both the archive and the language of the present moment for rendering transcendent experiences. Like Knox, Beckman reminds us, subtly and skillfully, of the distance between language and experience, the widening gap between the signifier and the "light" it gestures toward.

As the book unfolds, Beckman frequently calls attention to the ways language sustains this "continued darkness," this distance. By pairing phrases from vastly different lexicons and cultural milieu—indeed, "handsome drugs" appear alongside "billiards" and a speaker "dying of moonlight"—Beckman often evokes the ineffable, asking us to consider what will not, and cannot, be said in language. As in Knox's work, we are made to experience speech as a source of both wonder and melancholy, as the narrator persistently mourns the inability to give voice to sublime experience. For example, Beckman writes,

> They, lost, and to the
> touch of one another do go
> and to say such things
> in the grass plain of day
> gone long – to be comfortable
> or to lay there ruining one's clothes [...]

Here, and elsewhere in the collection, Beckman implements diction and syntax that call attention to their own historicity. Indeed, the caesuras midway through the first quoted line ("They, lost, and...") immediately create a measured, even dramatic, tone, which is amplified by the work's adept shift into third person (especially when considering the use of the pronoun "one"). Yet Beckman's decidedly contemporary diction creates a productive tension when paired with this formal syntax. This provocative disconnect, and myriad potential readings to which it gives rise, prompts one to consider the ways language accumulates (and abandons) possibility over time, and the difficulty of being "comfortable" in a syntax that is constantly multiplying and subtracting.

*   *   *

Lisa Olstein's *The Resemblance of the Enzymes of Grasses to Those of Whales is a Family Resemblance* also considers the ways that language exists in, and is transformed by, time. Presented as a linked sequenced of epistolary prose poems, Olstsein's poems address a mysterious figure named Whistle, who is at turns confidante and purveyor of an impending apocalypse. Indeed, this faultlessly crafted book is populated by "cities being torn down," "floods," and "waves of data from all directions," evoking both biblical plagues and the inherent violence of a digitized cultural landscape. Olstein's imagery, like her diction, creates an experience of time as elliptical, recursive, and circular, returning like a literary text to the same themes, symbols, and motifs. In many ways, the style of Olstein's prose poses a provocative challenge to prevailing notions of time as linear, a sanctum only for master narratives and teleological arguments. As Olstein herself observes, we have "lived according to the captors' time, waking, eating, sighing, sleeping out of sync with everyone around us."

She subtly implies, through her careful curation of imagery, that time retains a layered quality, its slow and soundless movement allowing us to see confluences, divergences, repetitions. For Olstein, it is language that accumulates, and transfigures, the materials of history, its "despair" and its "fire." By pairing "vitamins," "prescriptions," and "brittle lawns" with the wreckage of "empire," Olstein also suggests the possibility of transforming experience through our use of language. Indeed, she renders us suddenly and startlingly aware of the presence of history, its myriad upheavals and inequities, in our smallest linguistic choices. She writes, for example, in "Every Pastoral Is an Elegy,"

> I saw it happen, Whistle, what the billboards describe, I saw it begin, a noiseless slipping of the face beneath the surface, the silence of going under, and in this case by chance or by vigilance the awful invisibility was visible enough to be reversed by swift leap and wild grasp and then he was in my arms

again, Whistle, like a newborn gasping and because
he is mine, he is mine, he is mine, because on that
day he did not die, because my fear from him I try
to hide, because in the womb all sound is a kind of
music, I started singing.

Here, and throughout the collection, Olstein's diction drifts
between history (embodied by such phrases as "swift leap" and
"wild grasp") and modernity (for example, "what the billboards
describe…"). Much like Beckman and Knox, Olstein prompts
us to consider the ways in which we search the archive when the
language of the present moment falls short, particularly when
attempting to convey sublime experience, the "singing" of the
senses upon witnessing a transcendent moment. Yet Olstein also
upholds the necessity of transforming the archive, and in doing so,
transfiguring our definitions of beauty and possibility. She shows
us that the presence of history and empire in language "is visible
enough," rendering us suddenly aware of culture's machinery,
how the archive, when its "hallowed halls" are opened, cultivates
repetition – of "fear," "what we hope desperately never to find."
The apocalypse portrayed in this collection, then, is revealed as an
end to language as we know it, a "slippery bridge across we don't
know what," a bridge where we will find "crossing soon foreclosed."

TIME AS EMPIRE AND RESISTANCE:
ON RECENT WORK BY CHRISTOPHER KEMPF,
SHANE MCCRAE, & TOBY MARTINEZ DE LAS RIVAS

IN *TOTALITY AND INFINITY*, EMANUEL LEVINAS describes memory as a reversal of historical time. In the darkened rooms of the mind, events abandon their chronology, the grand narrative no longer fits together the way it should. Yet it is this unraveling that allows us to see each spectacle in sharper relief, to perceive confluences and repetitions, to construct a lovelier arc, a story that is more just and more true. To remember is always to take apart, and in doing so, one invents the possibility of new teleology.

Three recent collections of poetry consider this complex relationship between memory, narrative, and our thinking about time. Indeed, we have been taught to impose a linear progression, a clear sequencing of uncertainties and upheavals; in doing so, we imagine an end to history's infinite transformations. Christopher Kempf's *Late in the Empire of Men*, Shane McCrae's *In the Language of My Captor*, and Toby Martinez de las Rivas' *Terror* each question, with subtlety and grace, these linear models of time and history that have become all too familiar. Each volume offers a gorgeously fractured, elliptical narrative arc, what de la Rivas describes as a "razored Book of Hours."

In the work of Kempf, McCrae, and de las Rivas, we are reminded that it is possible to "dance" through time with "terrific abandon." Here, we are invited to imagine history's "brightest trajectory," which almost always gestures toward the "light & knowledge" that lie just beyond the lovely arc of story. These skilled and subtle writers remind us what narrative, with implied temporality and causation, can and cannot hold. As the intricate structure—that careful architecture—of each collection begins to reveal itself, we are left only with "terror that is all-abiding," the ruins of an empire we once thought we knew.

*   *   *

Kempf's *Late in the Empire of Men* takes the form of a book-length sequence of persona-driven lyrics, which consider the relationship between power, privilege, and various constructions of masculinity. The speakers of these carefully constructed poems range from "a man made of pixels" to an OK Cupid user who believes "love is plural." With that in mind, it is useful to think of Kempf's work not as advocacy, but rather, a documentary project, one that gathers and accounts for narratives circulating within a culture that is deeply flawed. In Kempf's deftly constructed sequence, masculinity and empire are revealed as a palimpsest that can never be fully or convincingly erased. We are reminded that the cultural moment we inhabit is in actuality a layering of past "cities" and their "music," an "excavation" taking place just below our conscious perceptions of which we are largely unaware. As Kempf himself reminds us, "everyone we know is asleep."

Throughout this stunning volume, time and its accompanying narratives fold in on themselves, as we drift from the "Information Age" to "the '90s," to "mythic" antiquity and back again. It is his circular movement through history and its discontents that allows us to see that inherited mistakes "are carried inside us like a seed," how we have internalized a century of missteps, a path that has essentially trapped us, like a "floodgates" or "a divine wind." For example, Kempf writes in "Sledding at the Harding Memorial,"

> ...& later that evening
> the team of men whose job it was rose
> from their dinners & lifted into place
> the great slab, something Paleolithic laid
> at the spot where history limped away
> to remember itself. & somewhere far
> below us our father watched...

Kempf's carefully curated imagery, the "great slab" of a "tomb" looming over the children as they sled on fresh snow, as well as the father's omnipresence in their play, evokes a present that contains within it the past. Indeed, Kempf fully acknowledges that we cannot simply exist outside of a shared cultural memory, as its implicit assumptions have been too deeply internalized. Yet Kempf also gestures toward the possibility of self-awareness, a path "cleared free of small boughs," a more cognizant navigation of history and the things we carry through its luminous gates. In many ways, this curation of cultural memory is the "spectacular *fin de siècle*," "the Bellagio" that lies just beyond what we are able to imagine in the language of empire.

*   *   *

Much like Kempf's work, McCrae's collection frames language as both intimacy and violation. Indeed, he reminds us that we rarely choose the grammar we inhabit, with its implicit causalities, hierarchies, and judgments. For McCrae, this kind of linguistic imperialism is the ultimate violence, as grammar structures conscious experience, determining what can and cannot be dreamed, what thoughts must remain "deep and far in darkness."

McCrae's volume, like *Late in the Empire of Men*, shows us that the present moment "memorializes" a history of linguistic dislocation while also bearing it indefinitely into the future, into the empty rooms of "no country we have seen." Indeed, one of the questions that drives the collection is whether one's life in language is a captivity that cannot be shaken.

Midway through the collection, McCrae introduces a powerful series of prose vignettes, which depict a child exploring an abandoned house. As the sequence unfolds, these unused rooms—replete with "furniture," "kitchen appliances," "toys," everything one would need to build a life—become an emblem for lost possibility, an existence outside the constricting language of empire. McCrae reminds us though, of the loneliness of this dream, as it is language—with all of its flaws and shortcomings—that makes possible community and shared experience. He elaborates,

> The houses and the warehouse were separated by about 100 feet of dirt, and patches of broken concrete, and thorny, low bushes, and grass. I call it a village, but there wasn't more to it than what I've just described. I call it a village because it was abandoned—the words seem to go together—and filled with trash and also things I thought people wouldn't have left behind, things that looked important to me…

In much the same way that the "village" with its "low thorny bushes" was "abandoned" years ago, filled with "things that looked important," McCrae's riveting speaker is haunted by a shadow community, and a shadow self, which both exist outside of language, with its residue of trauma and violence. The meadow and its echoing structures become a space for dreaming, an emblem for freedom, but this transcendence, too, is deeply problematic. McCrae reminds us that when one flees language and empire, there is no one on the other side to greet you.

*   *   *

Terror, too, considers the ways each word contains within it the world, its histories, and its upheavals. De las Rivas, however, takes this line of thinking in a slightly different direction, exploring the ways language can both inform and destabilize our thinking about time. Here, we are made to see that found text can uncenter narrative, unraveling its "brake of thorns," exhuming "the full range of its tragedy." Through carefully orchestrated juxtapositions and skillful shifts in register, de las Rivas reveals to us the "blue lustre" of antiquity in each syllable. As we drift between "the lyric" and its "formal counterpoint," we are finally able to see modernity, its "spite" and its "denials," in sharper relief. Indeed, the poems in

Terror render us startlingly aware of the many distinct empires and upheavals that inhabit each utterance, every word a "wide array twitched open" to reveal a kingdom, its "light-bearing rage." In such a way, de las Rivas challenges, subtly and masterfully, the familiar linear models of time and history. "The summer wind tilts in my mouth," he writes, "I cannot set one word down straight." As de las Rivas himself admits, it is markedly difficult to situate the work's language in any given temporal moment. His sentences are instead a ledger, tracing the speaker's movement through a vast, rich, and ultimately shared cultural memory. By bearing witness to the "raucous, oppositional light" contained in every speech act, de las Rivas calls our attention the violence implied by linear models of temporality, the erasure inherent in the creation of a master narrative. He writes, for example,

> Seventhly, I pray for the sparrow with a slashed tongue
> who in Egypt wore a jackal's garish blunt head
> & ferried dead children across the river, but in England
> he's a happy, fat fellow. I listen to his declining brotherhood at Broadway: there is one fewer every day.

Here, and elsewhere in the book, de las Rivas acknowledges the many ways that the language of an empire is internalized. One fashions an identity out of its teleologies, its implicit hierarchies and judgments. At the same time, he calls attention to changeability of language, geography, and as a result, concepts of identity. The sparrow, with its migration and flight, becomes an emblem for our place in a vast and inherently unstable linguistic terrain. In much the same way that "the sparrow" metamorphoses from a creature with "a slashed tongue" to a "fat, happy fellow," we are made to see the possibility of migrating within language, discovering new frameworks for organizing the world and our place within it. The "terror" evoked in the work's title, then, is not the captivity of described by McCrae, or the entrapment inherent in Kempf's master narratives, more like awe, the "wonder" and "shivering" when presented with infinite possibility.

REPETITION AS VOYAGE AND TRANSFIGURATION: ON RECENT WORK BY BEN LERNER, KRISTY BOWEN, AND ELIZABETH J. COLEN

I WAS INITIALLY RESISTANT TO BEN LERNER'S *Mean Free Path*. After all, he does warn the reader that there is "[n]othing for you here but repetition." The unvaried line-lengths of these poems, and the seemingly constrained vocabulary of imagery, could easily appear as mere remnants of a failure of the imagination. Yet we tend to forget that any transformation begins with reiteration, as the phrase we recall is said and unsaid, memorialized and unmade at the same time.

With that in mind, Lerner reminds his reader that there is no such thing as "sameness" when considering an encounter with the poetic image. As his speaker moves through time, and as he is changed by its articulation of history, he discovers each "star," each "identical city" with a different mind and heart. Lerner helps us see repetition as undeniable difference, as the "applause," and the "sedimented roar," are revisited on an individual who has fundamentally metamorphosed. We are made to hear his "voice" as both old and new, in much the same way that we are shown oneself as another.

Two other recent collections, Kristy Bowen's *Salvage* and Elizabeth J. Colen's *What Weaponry* offer startling variations on this framing of repetition as subtle transformation. In Bowen's gorgeously cinematic presentation of the poetic image, each "house made of mothers," each "house destroyed" functions as a projection, a portrait of a self that remains in a constant state of flux. We are shown ongoingness and becoming frame by frame, the poems functioning as stills of a heroine on screen, who never ceases moving. Similarly, Colen's recurrent imagistic motifs make provocative ontological claims. She calls our attention the ways that repetition is often a process of estrangement, as each iteration of the same image bears us further and further afield.

Taken together, these three books raise what is essentially a question of limitation and possibility: How much transfiguration can the same mind, and the same finite world, sustain?

*   *   *

In *Mean Free Path*, Lerner builds a "dark aisle" just to see how much "plain language" can fit within it without the door coming "unhinged." Each poem's construction represents both minimalistic restraint and egregious excess, as significance accumulates around every "disaster" revisited, every familiar and perilous "edge."

This notion of repetition as precarious architecture, as accumulation, and as necessary destruction, is enacted on both small and large scales. On the level of the individual poem, we see many very different types of repetition holding vastly divergent lines together. Taking the first poem after the dedication as an example, one observes sound (such as the alliteration that binds "delays" to "sensations," "audible" to "absence" and "rain"), as well as syntax (particularly the subject-verb-object construction that links clauses like "Waiting is the answer" and "Any subject will do") and of course, recurrent imagistic motifs.

These subtle gestures within each poem serve to mitigate the wild associative leaps that occur, as there are often ontological and syntactic worlds between one line (for example, "The audible absence of rain") and the next (meaning, the wildly divergent "Take the place of objects"). Repetition offers a way of closing gaps, but also, a way of transforming them, allowing each vast expanse bridged by "description" to become a "system," a "standing wave," enlivened by movement and slow, careful metamorphosis.

As these varied and various types of repetition intersect and overlap on the level of the larger sequence, their interlocking structure becomes metaphor, ultimately traversing the distance that is so elegantly described in these poems: "I'm writing this one/

With my eyes closed, listening to the absence of..." Indeed, the imagistic motifs, syntactic structures, and alliterative gestures that recur throughout the sequence, and that bind one line to the next, begin to simulate proximity, despite the syntactic and metaphoric chasms that separate each line, each poem, each page.

In many ways, it is this tension between distance and proximity that allows Lerner's framework to hold so many of the same "little contrasts" without becoming claustrophobic for the reader, as we are made to see each motif, each syntactic structure from different emotional and intellectual vantage points. As Lerner himself writes, "Nothing's changed except the key."

*   *   *

The most moving poems in Lerner's book are those that address the absent other directly: "If you would speak of love/Stutter, like rain..." It is this unflinching lyricism that allows us to understand that desire motivates these elaborate accumulations, the careful architecture that takes shape over the course of the book.

For Lerner, the love lyric becomes voyage and transfiguration, a landscape that is slowly and irrevocably transformed, just as the speaker is changed–by time, history, and the relationship itself. Lerner writes:

> You startled me. I thought you were sleeping
> In the traditional sense. I like looking
> At anything under glass, especially
> Glass. *You* called *me*. Like overheard
> Dreams...

Although the pronoun "you" is reiterated throughout these lines, we are presented with vastly different facets of the same love object: she is at turns secretive (as she "startles" the speaker), somnambulant ("I thought you were sleeping"), and finally disconnected, prompting both clarification and denial ("*You* called *me*"). Indeed, repetition subtly suggests that distance and proximity inhabit the same moments. With each reiteration of the word "glass," we find ourselves at a greater remove, one step further from the desired narrative. The layers of "glass" multiply, concealing a version of the scene that is possibly more real and more true. Just as the speaker "likes looking/At anything under glass/Especially glass," we see both characters refracted and distorted through repetition. Yet this distortion is revealed as the truest representation of the dynamic between them, the impossibility of empathy and connection, and the knowledge that one can never fully inhabit the mind or heart of another.

In many ways, the moments of indirectness within the collection allow us to see Lerner's more direct pieces in sharper relief. When the glass reappears, as rubble ("axes to grind into glass") and as threshold ("sliding doors," "a poem through a windshield") the speaker meets them alone.

*   *   *

Elizabeth J. Colen's *What Weaponry* offers a provocative variation on Lerner's envisioning of repetition as distance and proximity. For Colen, repetition is a process of making strange, bearing us farther and farther away from the familiar with each room revisited, each reiteration of the image we once thought we knew.

Much like *Mean Free Path*, *What Weaponry* utilizes many different types of repetition: parallel syntax, sound motifs, and of course, a vocabulary of imagery that imposes its own willful constraints. Here sound and syntax, however familiar they may become, only heighten the wonderful strangeness of Colen's imagery. She writes in "Low Clouds,"

> When we see it from above we will know the sea
> is near, as is the grey, as is the end. When we see
> it from above the plane will be circling, destroying

low clouds. When we see it from above we will be listening, we will be watching, we will go there as fast as we can.

The quoted poem, the first in the collection, reads almost as ars poetica, instructing the reader how to approach the "circling" and recursive prose within the book. Here "the sea," which appeared earlier in the poem as "wet sand between our toes," has been rendered entirely other, functioning as a harbinger of destruction. Indeed, what makes "the sea" and the "low clouds" so disconcerting is the vantage point from which they are seen as the poem draws to a close: we slowly realize that we are falling. As the poem's "concentric circles grow," each return, each reiteration is also a step toward the poem's unmaking. Though the "crabs" and "dry kelp" comprise a fairly consistent vocabulary of maritime imagery, the vantage point from which it is seen becomes less and less safe. In this respect, Colen's work proves comparable to Lerner's, as the same image is presented at varying degrees of remove. Repetition for both writers is a voyage, an orbit around a deceptively stable center of gravity.

* * *

What Weaponry is perhaps most powerful when this repetition becomes a kind of violence. Given the familiarity of the images and syntactic structures we encounter, this framing of the book's "talking in circles" as aggression, as threat is all the more unexpected. In this respect, repetition is not only a source of structural unity within the book, but a form of resistance, a sly and subtle feminist practice.

Throughout *What Weaponry*, we are presented with "mornings [that] stab the breath right out of our lungs." Yet the speaker of these poems is also implicated in this destruction, which she willfully and recklessly summons. The speaker's fascination with violence (and its relationship to the physical body) is enacted beautifully in Colen's presentation of fire. She writes, for example, in "The Perfect Kind of Happy,"

I hold your hand or I strike you or you strike me or light up a cigarette and our upstairs disappears. But what if we're in it? I think of particles exploding, coming back together like some physics experiment I don't know the name for. "Large Hadron Collider," you say.

Here Colen conflates the act of smoking with interpersonal violence ("I strike you...", "You strike me..."), suggesting that this kind of harm is also done slowly and unwittingly to oneself. At the same time, Colen subtly implies that aggression and conflict are built into the very "particles" that make us. For Colen, this "experiment" represents a necessary destruction, what may be conceived of as a generative kind of violence.

In many ways, the impact of this passage is heightened by repetition on a larger scale, as the small fire portrayed here ("lighting up a cigarette...") only grows with each provocative prose piece. Within a few pages, we are presented with "campfire," "an active volcano," and finally, "a face lighting up." The fire that Colen depicts in these passages becomes destruction and resistance, a threat to oneself and the other.

*   *   *

Salvage offers a provocative take on this framing of repetition as subtle violence, as necessary devastation. We are offered a vision of the self as inherently unstable, a self that is destroyed over and over again, only to emerge more luminous and more fierce. What's more, Bowen shows us the speaker's transfiguration frame by frame. This book-length sequence reads as deconstructed cinema, as a gorgeously fractured film reel.

Like Colen and Lerner, Bowen utilizes repetition not only as a source of unity and cohesion, but as metaphor, as ontological statement. Throughout Salvage, voice is borne out of the destruction of a self who is not yet past, singing towards a future that has not yet materialized. This Hegelian notion of transformation as destruction, and time as inevitable violence, is perhaps most visible in Bowen's sequence, "dreams about houses and bees." Here the reader is presented with infinite variations on the same image, a house that is at turns "four-chambered" and "falling," that doubles as a "museum of unruly saints." Bowen's use of repetition here it twofold: we are offered a consistent vocabulary of domestic imagery, certainly, but each poem retains a subtle variation on what appears at first to be the same title, with its familiar syntactic construction: "House made of…. or "House which is…" Each "house which is a kind of falling," and each "house of misused potential" functions as a projection, a rendering of the speaker's emotional and psychic topography, which is inevitably externalized.

Bowen writes in "house made of ghosts and small animals,"

> For every love song, there is a broken dove skeleton
> rotting in the eaves. A leaving, that requires
> nothing but the door opening and closing just once.
> A heaviness of suitcases and floor lamps and
> record albums piled awkwardly in the trunk.

The speaker's interior drama, the "longing" and cruel "motives" that exist simultaneously, are enacted in the objects she chooses to populate the domestic space: "love songs" at odds with "broken dove skeletons," the lightness music coupled with the "heaviness" of her personal affects. Here we are presented with a space marked by tension, the speaker's desire for multiple and contradictory outcomes. In many ways, Bowen's rendering of this domestic space is all the more startling, considering the poem immediately before, its rooms populated by "love letters" and "tiny glass kittens."

As the reader wanders the halls of this "house of beautiful drownings," we see a slow transformation of the speaker projected onto the space she inhabits. Through her seamless and artful repetition, Bowen calls our attention to the relationship between time and the rooms we traverse, as each "house of strays," each "house of open wounds" documents a self that is already and irrevocably past.   I find myself deeply moved by Bowen's work when she acknowledges temporality as violence, as necessary destruction. In many ways, it its this repetition with a slight difference allows her entry to this ambitious philosophical question.

Salvage is aptly named, as Bowen gracefully and articulately gathers the fragments of each burned house, each broken window. Like Colen and Lerner, Bowen shows us that when we try to hold on to the things we have accumulated - "salt shakers, salad forks, tiny match books"- it's really the space between our fingers that lets the light through.

"LETTING THEM STAY, IN SOME MEASURE, UNKNOWN":
AFFECT & THE OBJECT WORLD
IN TWO RECENT HYBRID TEXTS

RECENT YEARS HAVE SEEN A RESURGENCE of interest in archival material among creative practitioners. Indeed, these excavations of our literary and cultural past range from rigorous scholarly engagement – as is the case with Janet Holmes' unearthing of Dickinson's activist poetics in *THE MS OF MY KIN* – to the deeply personal exploration of family history - and the political structures that define such narratives - in Jill Magi's *THREADS*. Yet the archive often remains purely in the realm of the textual, appearing as a storehouse of language, rich with the weight of meanings accrued over time.

Two recent hybrid works, Karen Green's *BOUGH DOWN* and Jennifer Moxley's *THERE ARE THINGS WE LIVE AMONG: ESSAYS ON THE OBJECT WORLD*, ultimately challenge the limitations inherent in our operative definitions of textual history. Both Moxley and Green present us with an archival practice that is based in the object world, suggesting that material artifacts, too, bear the weight of centuries. In these provocative works, the artifact becomes a locus for the ongoing generation of narrative, as each luminous hairpin, and each bright postage stamp, is revealed as a small glittering part in a larger cultural machinery.

Though vastly different in form and approach, Karen Green's *BOUGH DOWN* and Jennifer Moxley's *THERE ARE THINGS WE LIVE AMONG* share an investment in showing - through the lives of objects, and the wildly divergent significances that we attach to them - how culture's shared consciousness unfolds over time. Each sequence of prose texts functions as a kind of ledger, accounting for the movements of seemingly small artifacts in an ever-widening imaginative topography. In these finely crafted collections, meaning accrues around an "antique nightgown," a "kerosene lamp" as the world changes shape, ultimately failing to bear these once necessary items into the luminous present. Moxley and Green remind us that we turn to narrative as a way to close this gap, to bind past and present, to reconcile incipient with obsolete.

*   *   *

Moxley's THERE ARE THINGS WE LIVE AMONG functions as a dazzling accumulation, as histories are layered upon alternate and often conflicting histories. In this sense, the work also serves as an enactment of the very nature of the artifact itself, as each provocative prose piece appears as merely a moment in a shared psychic terrain that extends indefinitely.

For Moxley, the history of an object is also a history of its life in language. Indeed, her meditation on the object world inevitably turns to other narratives, among them Marcel Proust's body of work, George Oppen's "Of Being Numerous," and *Robinson Crusoe*. Through her wondrous survey of past literature, Moxley shows us that consciousness is but the generation of narrative, and the "things we live among" are its very machinery, the train bears us gracefully into story and memory. For example, she notes that "[a]fter Robinson Crusoe washes up on his 'Island of Despair,' the meagerness of his possessions drive him into temporary madness." Here Moxley subtly calls our attention to the inextricable relationship between the material and the textual. To lose one's possessions, however unremarkable they may be, is to lose a link to language, and to the unfolding of conscious experience.

In many ways, this relationship between the material and the ongoing text of the mind is enacted beautifully in her brief essays on shoes. The unadorned and humble "clog" becomes a nexus for systemic inequalities and the violence that they often beget. Moxley writes, citing Robert Bresson's filmography, that the heroine's "huge ill-fitting clogs…seem both defiant, as she drags her feet, and restraining, as if an emblem of her oppressive

57

situation, her poverty, and her obvious, indelicate sexuality." Here each loosed thread, each drably colored swatch of fabric contains within it the world – along with its elaborate power structures and inequities. A made thing is revealed as a projection of the human body, as well as the accompanying constructions of gender, race, and class that determine its place in a larger economy of language, texts, and goods.

Indeed, Moxley shows us that the humble clog becomes palimpsest, inscribed with history's seismic shifts, a narrative which is then erased and written over again. The shoe later appears emblem of femininity and again as fetish item, as a darkening horizon that "lets fall a torrent." In many ways, this onslaught could be read as a description of the text itself, the accumulation of discrete, self-contained narratives around an alluringly absent center. Each seemingly unremarkable object serves as a point of entry to an imaginative topography that is borne away as soon as we enter it.

*   *   *

Much like Moxley's collection of linked essayistic hybrids, Green's prose texts examine the world of things as a language in itself. Yet Green takes this assertion a step farther, exploring the ways material artifacts – a brightly colored postcard, a stamped envelope – can convey what is unspeakable in language proper.

As one might expect, the images contained within Green's BOUGH DOWN are governed by a kind of grammar, always surrounded by white space, always implying a very particular variety of silence. Narrative falls away, allowing the object world to speak in its stead. Each image is housed by its own luminous and ghostly white page. Narrative and image are coeval, but never co-conspirators, existing somewhat separately, though illuminating one another from that small and necessary distance.

What's more, image becomes narrative, evoking memory and

its elaborate, luminous corridors. The collection begins with a fragmentary list of details – time ("June") and color ("black"), "pills," the "latch" on the door, and "prayers." When an image does appear – blurred text on a background of more text, handwritten and typeset, precise and imprecise – its palimpsestic quality becomes a commentary on the narrative proper. Green suggests, through her skillful juxtaposition, that mourning is more than anything a loss of language. The signs we have come to rely on lose their meaning; we try but cannot make sense out of them.

When Green prompts us to reenter language proper, we are equipped with a new awareness of the text and its terms of engagement. The prose entries that follow are populated by a "jazz lady," the narrator's beloved (deceased) husband, and a luminous, distant past. The loss of speech, represented just before, is revealed as a refusal of time and its movements. The recursive structure of the text speaks to and with the image that we've just seen, suggesting that the ability to communicate depends on our acceptance of temporality, its inherent limitations.

Here image is text, a grammar and a lexicon in and of itself. Like Moxley, Green works to expand the boundaries of the archive, and the poet's place within it. Both BOUGH DOWN and THERE ARE THINGS WE LIVE AMONG are carefully considered, provocative works, which inhabit the rich tradition of archival poetry while at the same time challenging, revising, and interrogating it.

LANDSCAPE AND SORROW
IN THREE EXPERIMENTAL TEXTS

IN MUCH OF CONTEMPORARY POETRY, landscape becomes a convenient vehicle for dramatizing the inner life of the speaker. And so the florid hills that surround us, with their clean lines and small enclosures, serve as a simple metonymy for complex emotional and intellectual discoveries. What's more, these narratives are related to us from a distance, their pastoral mode offering a method for dealing with affect at some degree of remove.

Three recent collections of poetry are a rare exception to this disconcerting trend in contemporary poetry. Lisa Robertson's *The Weather*, Lindsey Tigue's *System of Ghosts*, and Emily Abendroth's *Exclosures* do not merely consider landscape as a dramatized descriptive strategy. Instead, the progression of the book-length sequence is synonymous with the creation of a rich linguistic and psychic terrain. Certainly, the pastoral mode provides a vocabulary for sketching these beautiful and treacherous textual expanses. Yet the work of building this imaginative topography is not done through exposition, but rather, it is accomplished by each sequence's innovative and singular form.

Indeed, Abendroth, Tigue, and Robertson each present us with structures as alive with sound as they are with emotion, poems as unruly on the printed page as any true wilderness. To experience each book, the reader must fully inhabit a luminous and skillfully constructed architecture. The end result is not a simple extended metaphor, but rather, a richly imagined world—in which language, mind, landscape are inextricably bound—and in which the reader is fully and willingly engulfed.

*   *   *

In Abendroth's *Exclosures*, experimentation with form serves to create a textual terrain that is constantly expanding. This gesture may be read in part as a metaphor for the speaker's affect as she grieves a political structure that is unraveling before her. Yet Abendroth also prompts us to consider the ways landscape becomes tangled in multiple (and often incommensurable) societal infrastructures.

She writes, for example, in "Exclosure 9,"

> "The [Onsite check-cashing franchise] does not have
> a monopoly on exclusionary logistics."
> [Elk's Club]
> [Offshore Military Base]
> [Nuclear Family]
> [Academic Community]
> [Bail Bonds Market]
> [Single Professionals Network]
> [Sensor-Activated Motion Detector]

The landscape that the speaker traverses is borne into the machinery of surveillance, commerce, and social life. Through her intricately tiered lineation, Abendroth reveals the multiplicity housed within any given physical space. Certainly, one might read this poem as an exercise in choice, in which we sort through the various options with which we are presented ("Elk's Club," "Offshore Military Base," etc.). Abendroth's poems, however, prove to be a much more complex constructions. She prompts us to consider the various types of cultural machinery that overlap and intersect in any given terrain.

Here, the infrastructure of "national security" casts a dim shadow over the "nuclear family," and echoes as Abendroth bears it in language. Similarly, the jargon of the "academic community" is portrayed in discomfiting proximity to poverty's looming architectures. There is no longer any single topography, but multiple courses being charted within the same physical space. For Abendroth, inhabiting any terrain also involves negotiating the structures of power and authority that are enacted within its boundaries.

Indeed, the linguistic topography of *Exclosures* is more palimpsest than pastoral, as Abendroth inscribes, erases, and reinscribes the structures of power and powerlessness, voicelessness and protest. In doing so, she reminds us, "There's no combination that isn't mutually contagious."

* * *

Lindsey Tigue's *System of Ghosts* offers a similar unearthing of the economic and political infrastructures that inform our experience of physical spaces. Presented as a sequence of skillfully linked individual poems, the collection returns again and again to the question of solitude, the ways that urban industrial modernity can render a landscape suddenly and startlingly desolate. On the level of the sequence, the architecture of the collection enacts the depersonalizing economic system that is being described, each piece functioning as a small shimmering gear in a larger textual machine.

In many ways, this notion of poem as system, language as commercialized landscape, is enacted in Tigue's artful transitions from one poem to the next. She writes, for instance, at the end of "Solitary, Imaginary,"

> I act like I'm not thrilled, that I don't love
> to meet neighbors in the street. *Do you*
> *have power?* I ask. *Do you have light?*

Here technology's failure is synonymous with the emergence of a community. Tigue makes it clear, however, that this power outage offers only a brief respite from "claimed settlements" and "trucks unloading." This piece leads seamlessly into "How to Adjust Time Zones," a lyric exploration of how technology has fragmented our sense of temporality, space, and relationships. She writes,

> Before the railroad,
> People based time

on the natural
movement of the sun.

Now, my sister lives
two hours behind me.

Though technology connects us in spite of our geographic distance,
it also propels us further into isolation, each individual inhabiting
a singular and solitary psychic landscape. What is perhaps most
fascinating about this collection is the way it simultaneously enacts
and resists the systematization that is being described.

Like Abendroth's *Exclosures*, the book provocatively calls attention
to itself as a commodity, interrogating the circumstances of its
own making. The reader, too, is implicated in sustaining this
dangerous machinery.

*   *   *

Robertson's collection ultimately resists this impulse to treat
language as commodity, as an object to be bought and sold.
Indeed, there is nothing quite as non-utilitarian as the weather.
Perhaps for this reason, Robertson's *The Weather* emulates this very
impracticality, offering us language as atmosphere, as ambient
sound. The end result is a textual terrain that resists semantic
meaning, as this mindset represents a desire for language to remain
merely serviceable.

Robertson's rhythmic meaning-making, and her engagement with
language as a raw material, results in a dangerous proliferation
of possibility, similar to Abendroth's ever-expanding textual
dreamscapes. Much like the weather itself, the shifting possibilities
of Robertson's imaginative topography prove to be as treacherous
as they are enlivening. She writes,

Cheerful, tender, civil, lilac colours; we anticipate

the never-the-less. Clear blue but yellowish in the northeast; we sit and explore. Clouded toward the south; we will not be made to mean by a space. We'll do newness. Crickets accumulate; our expression of atmosphere has carnal intentions…

Here Robertson conceives of language as a material medium, allowing the alliterative music of "Cheerful, tender, civil, lilac colours" to create the same ambient and immersive atmosphere as the "clouded" skies and "clear blue" backdrop that she describes. As the weather inevitably shifts, so too does Robertson's linguistic rendering of its movements. "A very wet day" turns to an "alibi," "a church," and later, the "sun situated just so."

At the end of the sequence, we are left with only one imperative: "go as the robin / as the songsparrow go / as the robin as the song." As Robertson ushers her linguistic tapestry into an even more sweeping terrain, we are reminded that it is language that gives structure to landscape, that lends music and meaning to that "anarchy," that "untranslatability," that "din."

"THE HEART GROWS STRANGER": SORROW & THE UNSPEAKABLE IN THREE RECENT PROSE TEXTS

IN *BLACK SUN*, JULIA KRISTEVA OBSERVES that mourning is, in essence, a loss of language. Words abandon their meaning; sentences no longer fit together the way they should. Yet it is language that allows us to derive significance from an experience, integrating it into our understanding of the world around us. The sorrow of a lost object, then, is a double loss: the thing itself has vanished and so too has its place in the lovely arc of story. Once we have fallen out of language, the absence itself becomes unspeakable, and likewise, the stories that makes us ourselves.

Three recent hybrid texts explore, with subtlety and grace, this troubled relationship between grief and the various structures of meaning making that we have inherited: grammar, narrative, their implied causalities, and their inherent limitations when faced with misfortune. We attempt to impose the logic of story, the clean reasoning of the sentence, when there is no satisfying causal relationship to be found. Indeed, Allison Benis White's *Please Bury Me in This*, Yanara Friedland's *Uncountry: A Mythology*, and Spring Ulmer's *The Age of Virtual Reproduction* offer a provocative disconnect between their pristine prose paragraphs and the fitting fragmentation of meaning found within them. We are reminded of what it is to be rendered "wordless," with only the "thin clothes" of narrative to cover our grief.

In the work of White, Friedland, and Ulmer, we are made to witness language as it reaches for something that lies just beyond its boundaries. Here, we are offered "glass beads" and "paper houses," "swans" and "paintings of windows" that orbit around an alluringly absent center. The reader is subtly and skillfully implicated in their desire for the story as memento, as "silver, gleaming" keepsake. Yet as sentences begin to assemble themselves in fits and starts, the speakers of these gorgeously fractured poems are left only with "words, their spectacular lack."

*   *   *

White's *Please Bury Me in This* takes the form of prose epistles, though the terms of address are constantly shifting. In many ways, the book's dedication is key to understanding a provocatively destabilized variation on the lyric: *for the four women I knew who took their lives within a year / for my father.* The speaker's grief uncenters her. Voice is revealed as a social construct, predicated on the existence of relationships; without the presence of the other, one struggles to speak. "I want to tell you something memorable," White writes, "something you could wear around your neck." Yet this stunning collection does much more, confronting instead the philosophical problems inherent in our desire to memorialize the lost other in language.

As the speaker drifts between remembered scenes, rooms, and objects, the work's neatly constructed prose stanzas prove deceptive, yet purposefully so. For the reader, prose evokes a variety of readerly expectations: unity of voice, consistency of address, and a readily apparent narrative arc. We have been trained to expect artifice: the "a string of glass beads wrapped several times around" the heroine's neck, "a napkin folded into a swan," then "yet another beautiful thing." Approached with that in mind, the work's fractured, ambulatory structure surprises and delights with its verisimilitude, especially when considering the actual workings of the mind when engulfed by grief.

> *And years later, deliriously, when he was dying, Do you have the blood flower?*
>
> *I was taught to chant 'he loves me, he loves me not' as I tore off each petal in my room.*
>
> *You are not alone in your feeling of aloneness. Yes, I have the blood flower.*

White, fittingly and deftly, offers only the illusion of wholeness. Certainly the prose in this passage appears in cleanly reasoned sentences, each subject-verb-object construction implying its own discrete causal chain. Yet within this seemingly linear, seemingly rational structure, White skillfully, and provocatively, fractures time. The "torn petals" and innocent "chant" of the speaker's childhood are held in the mind alongside her later efforts to reach beyond the scope of language and voice: *You are not alone...* This fragmentation of time and narrative, and this layering of discrete temporal moments, calls attention to the artifice of the various frameworks we attempt to impose upon experience. These often linear, often causal ways of creating order from disparate perceptions ultimately fall short of accounting for the ontological violence to which we are all subjected, inevitably. For White, what is truly meaningful resides in the aperture between two words, the threshold between rooms in "the museum of light."

*   *   *

Spring Ulmer's *The Age of Virtual Reproduction* engages similar questions of language and grief, albeit on a larger scale. The work offers a provocative and timely exploration of cultural memory and shared consciousness in the digital age, prompting the reader to consider the changing nature of mourning in a technologized social landscape. Carefully and convincingly grounded in the writings of Walter Benjamin, August Sander, and John Berger, Ulmer's work provocatively resists the language and structures of theory, seeking instead to create a more personal lexicon for sorrow and the visible fragmentation of culture and community.

Wonderfully associative in their logic and narrative progression, the linked essays in this collection depict the "fire" and "bullet-shattered glass" of shared mourning while refusing the impulse to weave a master narrative. In many ways, Ulmer's subtle protest, her linguistic resistance, comes across most visibly in the moments of rupture between neatly constructed, seemingly well-reasoned, sentences. Much like White, Ulmer upholds the importance of silence, and the space between words, for deriving meaning from the "played tricks" and "moral…anesthesia" that surround us. She writes in "Peasants,"

> They wear suits. Someone once remarked that they do not seem to fit them—their bodies cannot be tailored. I find their unfitted wear beseeching. I want them in these ill-fitting suits, enjoying their outing, looking so ephemeral. It is as if they never stopped for a picture. History cannot remember their names, just their bodies…

As in many passages in *The Age of Virtual Reproduction*, Ulmer's narrator mourns the once clear path to an ethical life. Here the photo, and the perceived innocence of the individuals in "ill-fitting suits," belies the speaker's nostalgia for what she perceived as a less conflicted social landscape. What's perhaps most telling, though, is the rupture between each sentence, the sudden leap from one idea to the next. Though longing for a beautiful past, in which everyone seems at once "beseeching" and charmingly vulnerable, the speaker has clearly internalized the values of the digital age. To move from the suits in the photo to the shortcomings of the human body (which "cannot be tailored") implies a hierarchy, privileging the made thing, the consumer good, over what is human. Ulmer's swift transitions, subtly and powerfully, implicate her own narrator, suggesting that these values no longer warrant justification. In this way, Ulmer's cultural critique, her grief when faced with cultural and political loss, is rendered all the more powerful by the style of her writing. What has been mislaid, for Ulmer, is an ethical sensibility, a moral narrative that once populated the space between actions, the pause between two words.

*　　*　　*

Much like White and Ulmer, Friedland calls our attention to what's left unsaid, and what cannot be said, in a narrative. *Uncountry: A Mythology* is presented as a series of self-contained flash fictions, which document, in luminous and lyrical fragments, a history of political exile. Often drifting between biblical narratives and twentieth century politics, Friedland offers a model of time and history that is circular and elliptical. We are pulled again and again towards the same sorrow, a grief that is deeply rooted in a shared cultural memory.

As *Uncountry* progresses, we are made to see that the grief accompanying a lost political struggle, the grief of nationhood, is greater than the individual that bears it. It is a "dark chamber," a "sea" that is constantly widening within the individual psyche. Friedland writes, for example, in "History of Breath,"

> Above the fireplace, which is never lit, his face during wartime. Full uniform, legs crossed, face in half profile against a wall of windows. On the table next to him a plant, cup saucer, a hunched angel in bronze...

What's perhaps most telling about this passage is its purposeful ambiguity. We are presented with archetypes of a mythic quality – the "half profile" of the soldier in "full uniform, legs crossed," the "hunched angel in bronze." In much the same way that Friedland forgoes specificity in description, so too the narrative drifts between wars and exiles, which slowly accumulate, one superimposed over the other. In many ways, it is this refusal of singularity that is one of the most powerful techniques that Friedland has at her disposal. By unsaying the particular, and denying the purported uniqueness of each sorrow, she gestures toward the presence of a larger cultural machine, which ceaselessly replicates archetypes, myths, mistakes. Much like White's gorgeously elusive prose, and Ulmer's wild associative leaps, Friedland's stately and mythic micro-narratives are perhaps most powerful in their silences. She reminds us to examine the space between words, the ethical implications of all what cannot, and will not, be said.

*   *   *

If mourning is a loss of language and narrative, perhaps that silence can be brought to bear on its own provocation. In the work of White, Ulmer, and Friedland, mourning, and its accompanying quiet, is no longer a passive endeavor. Rather, one's alienation from language, its implied order and structure, becomes pure possibility, a source of transformation, wonder and insight.

These three collections show us that silence can be made to speak on behalf of the lost other, perhaps even more powerfully than the familiar and ready-made structures of narrative. In each book, we are made to witness the underlying logic and assumptions of language as they are unsaid, and in this unsaying, we see them, suddenly, finally, and irrevocably, anew.

THE POETICS OF DISBELIEF

In 1817, Samuel Taylor Coleridge famously coined the term "suspension of disbelief," meaning, a willingness to silence one's critical faculties and believe in something purely conjectural for the sake of art. Since the publication of Coleridge's *Biographia Literaria*, his provocative ideas about cognitive estrangement – and the claim that we can so easily abandon the rules that govern our minds and hearts – have become indispensible for our understanding of how we experience works of literature. For Coleridge, some degree of trust in the storyteller, and a willingness on the part of the reader to take risks, is essential for a work of literary art to fully realize its aesthetic potential, to convey its meaning, and to assert its effects on the spectator.

In two recent hybrid texts, Coleridge's seminal writings on the "suspension of disbelief" are brought to bear on provocative and necessary sociopolitical questions. Paige Ackerson-Kiely's *dolefully, a rampart stands* and Sara Veglahn's *The Ladies* interrogate the structures of power that determine which narratives, and which storytellers, have the privilege of an unwavering trust, that startling absence of skepticism. In the work of these visionary writers, disbelief is revealed as a show of power and, more often than not, an all too familiar unwillingness to empower others.

Both Ackerson-Kiely and Veglahn share an investment in shining light on the politics implicit in disbelief, and examining its entrenched place in our culture as a tool of disempowerment. This impulse comes through most visibly in the relationship that these writers create between the text and its audience. As their work unfolds, they confront a kind of readerly disbelief, that tacit assumption that female practitioners will be rewarded for certain types of narratives, those stories of love, distress, and triumph that are familiar and culturally legible, while other narratives – and modes of narration - are supposedly suspect. As Ackerson-Kiely herself writes, "I wrote a victim impact statement the way I'd want to hear it."

Ackerson-Kiely's *dolefully, a rampart stands* sketches a landscape in which sexism and economic oppression are indelibly linked. Though her gorgeously rendered lines are filled with female speakers and women characters, the narratives themselves are marked by a striking contentiousness, as Ackerson-Kiely evokes the ways culture divides individuals from historically marginalized groups against themselves, if only to prevent them from rising up.

Ackerson-Kiely reveals the ways that power, censorship, and disbelief are internalized, as they live with us in our most solitary moments, and they circumscribe what is possible within our dreaming. In doing so, she challenges many of the myths of a shared feminist consciousness. For instance, she writes in "Book About a Candle Burning in a Shed,"

> I don't mention the dreams: Roadkill comes back to life, the answers I don't have but am asked for by an angry mob. What we do with details is not unlike touching a thing that doesn't want to be touched, a thing that would wheel around and bite the hand if only it could. The part of hunger we deserve.

*   *   *

The speaker, whose community has borne witness to so much violence, ultimately resists the invitation to narrate it in her own voice, preferring instead the "crackle and splinter" of a distant radio. The disbelief that inhabits this fictive town has been gradually internalized, becoming a deep silence, not unlike the "river that moves a body toward its banks."

In Ackerson-Kiely's presentation, this silence and self-censorship arises from an abiding suspicion surrounding women's voices, and stories that fail to adhere to familiar ideas how a life unfolds. In this fictive terrain, master narratives like these are as subtle as they are pervasive. "I know what you're thinking right now," Ackerson-Kiely writes in "Laconia," "It's true she took her first job after high school. What can you do." Here, and the throughout the book, she reacts against the assumptions that the reader likely brings to the poem, their belief that they can situate images, archetypes, and symbols within a framework culled from a shared cultural memory. Though acknowledging the familiar features of the story, Ackerson-Kiely does not want us to limit what is possible within it. "You were given everything," she tells the reader in "Meadow Redaction." Now they will learn be a good steward of the gift.

*   *   *

Veglahn's *The Ladies* continues this interrogation of disbelief and its implicit power dynamics. She shows us, subtly and skillfully, that the boundaries between self and other, and the perceived ownership of language and narrative, are often a precondition for readerly belief. Presented as a polyphonic text, in which a mysterious "we" plans, documents, and sings a revolution into being, the story takes as one of its central questions the relationship between the individual and the collective.

Within Veglahn's richly imagined text, the women's voices that comprise the chorus, the luminous "us" that populates these discrete prose episodes, never break away from the group. As the story unfolds, one begins to wonder whether they are encountering a multitude, or a self that contains within it multitudes. Like Ackerson-Kiely, Veglahn gestures at the ways shared culture, and its implicit power dynamics, give rise to a consciousness that is, at its core, divided.

Veglahn writes,

In the chapels. In the cathedrals. In the small

country churches. In the basements of churches. In
their rooms in the dark. In their kitchens. In their
doorways and hallways. Inside our heads. In our
minds, they spoke. They spoke through us. We do
not know how to explain this. It was not like voices.
It was not like thought.

Here Veglahn confronts and reacts against the readerly assumption
of a unified self, a self that can claim ownership over his or her
place in language. She resists this kind of textual ownership as
a precondition for belief, that willing suspension of skepticism.
"Inside our chests something was burning," Veglahn tells us,
"We couldn't identify what it was. We couldn't get it out."
Like Ackerson-Kiely, Veglahn makes the reader suddenly and
startlingly aware of the limitations they places on language before
it has a chance to unfold before them. For both Ackerson-Kiely
and Veglahn, it is the master narrative, that "small container,"
that limits the possibilities for belief, trust, and the creation of
community.

If univocal utterance is a precondition for readerly belief, then
what of the storyteller that contains within her the world? How
do we create fictions when our voices have been halved by a flawed
culture, its abuses of power, and their inevitable internalization?
For Veglahn and Ackerson-Kiely, seeing, and fully acknowledging,
these rifts and fissures is a first step toward change. These gifted
writers, through their experimentation with poetic voice and
readerly participation, remind us that a leap of faith can open up
rooms within what we once thought was a single room – a chapel
of light that has been there all along.

AUTHORITY AND REBELLION IN FEMINIST POETRY

Excerpt: In recent collections, poets Anne Champion, Carla Harryman, and Cate Peebles invoke familiar literary forms only to reframe them as vehicles for feminist critique.

In *Paper Machine*, Jacques Derrida asserts that he "believe[s] in the value of the book, which keeps something irreplaceable, and in the necessity of fighting to secure its respect." He frames the act of writing as both homage and destruction, a simultaneous dismantling and preservation of literary convention—after all, artists choose what traditions are truly "irreplaceable" and bear them into the future, while discarding other aspects of their artistic inheritances. These choices, for many writers, are what instigate that "fight to secure respect," the recognition of a work as being part of a lineage, despite the violence the author has done to it.

Three recent poetry collections do justice to the complex relationship between artistic tradition, perceived legitimacy, and rebellion: Anne Champion's *The Good Girl is Always a Ghost*, Carla Harryman's *Sue in Berlin*, and *Thicket* by Cate Peebles invoke familiar literary forms—namely couplets, tercets, and pristine prose paragraphs—only to reframe them as vehicles for feminist critique. Rather than discarding tradition altogether, these three gifted writers have chosen to summon the authority of an artistic lineage only to rebel.

In many ways, this disruptive impulse is most visible in these writers' handling of the familiar. Because we are deceived by a text that looks like what we know, we are willing to follow its author to the very periphery of what can be said with language. In such a way, an outmoded artistic repertoire is made to house truly provocative assertions about language, gender, and their relationship to the female body. As Champion herself notes, "The finest thing a woman can wear is her untethering."

*   *   *

Champion's *The Good Girl is Always a Ghost* harnesses a vast range of forms—among them couplets, tercets, quatrains—from a mostly male literary tradition. As the book unfolds, these vestiges of literary convention are utilized to comment on the containment of women's voices, their bodies, and their sexuality. Presented as a series of persona poems in the voices of female historical figures, or epistles directly addressed to them, Champion's work is immediately reminiscent of Julianna Baggott's *Lizzie Borden In Love: Poems in Women's Voices* and Kara Candito's *Taste of Cherry*, among many other feminist texts.

The poems in Champion's collection span the full range of histories, regimes, and cultural milieu—the icons engaged include Marilyn Monroe, Eva Braun, Anne Frank, Rose Parks, Judy Garland, Jackie Kennedy—and a wide variety of themes, but the work is unified by the friction that exists between form and content. Champion calls our attention to the ways these women's voices resist the strictures of convention, and the language itself strikes sparks against its seemingly orderly presentation. She writes in "Eva Braun, Mistress to a Monster":

> Politics, such things are men's concerns.
> The wolf loves me because I don't threaten
> authority. The wolf loves me painted pretty
>
> and demure – the weaker I am, the more
> he loves…

Here, Champion's lineation is especially telling. As she transitions from "I don't threaten" to "authority," the syntactic unit is literally halved, suggesting that the speaker does in fact maintain the potential to disrupt, to challenge, and to do violence to the established order. But the stanza break between "painted pretty" and "and demure" suggests the speaker's hesitation, a bit of uncertainty and interior drama surrounding her traditional female role.

Though highly skilled with respect to her use of inherited forms, Champion often chooses the most poignant moments to break the patterns she's established with respect to lineation, the length of stanzas, and the breadth of her lines. She writes in "Eva Peron,"

> Don't ask me what they worshipped in this
>   disintegrating   body,   my   heartbeat   like
> skipping
>   stones across a lake. I used to love
> like a woman
> famished, take men like a slingshot, like the bed
>   was nothing but a sky without a trace of
> storm.

Champion's jagged margins evoke the speaker's own restlessness within her "disintegrating body," which the poem's neat tercets ultimately fail to contain. The book is filled pieces like this one, in which familiar forms are subtly varied, whether through the visual presentation of the work on the page, an irregular margin, or an abrupt end mid-couplet or mid-tercet. Champion writes, as though reflecting on this repertoire of inherited form, "I can't understand this machine / of grief, its solitary gears, its churning, its malfunctions."

In *Thicket*, Peebles continues Champion's provocative meditation on the ways language and artistic convention work to contain women's voices, exploring the ways that inherited forms, and even grammar, lend an artificial sense of order to disruptive narratives and experiences. Presented as a series of short-lined poems and prose boxes with wide margins, Peebles ultimately uses these familiar forms to create a sense of claustrophobia on the part of the reader. These seemingly innocuous couplets and prose boxes are made to house critiques—of their limitations, their arbitrary nature, and their implicit politics.

Peebles writes, for example, at the beginning of the collection:

> Before or after the great wind storm that winter
> when all the oaks at Versailles were ripped
>
> by their hoary roots & thrown over the grounds
> like mottled cadavers, before or after the century turned,
>
> before we returned from abroad & moved forward...

By setting the poem in Versailles, Peebles gestures at the unacknowledged privilege inherent in the artistic tradition she has inherited, and continues to inhabit through her use of received forms. At the same time, the speaker's voice seems to resists the orderly structure of the poem's couplets as she recounts what are truly disruptive sensory experiences ("mottled cadavers" and the "hoary roots" of oaks, to name only a few discomfiting images). When considering the rhythms of the poem, the line seems to exist in tension with the syntactic unit, perhaps as a way of gesturing at the inherent artifice of the form and the manner in which we attempt to give structure to an incongruous and unruly experience of the world around us.

As the work unfolds, the "thicket" emerges as a metaphor for language itself. The work's central question, then, revolves around the nature of change, and the creation of a more just structure for shared communications. In other words, is it possible to inhabit a forest, whether literal or conceptual, that is ultimately violent and threatening? Can we create something new there without tearing down what is old? As Peebles herself writes, "When the flood comes / we will be on our phones / searching for how to save ourselves."

As the book unfolds, Peebles upholds the dialogue between tradition and innovation as a new frontier for many feminists. She writes near the end of the collection:

> I don't know exactly
> what real life is like: I know there are men posed,
>
> contrapost, in perpetual reward; jars of dynasty's
> hearts and spleens; all matter of admissions to
>
> the netherworld – a body in a box & the box
> in a box in a chest in the ground.

Like Champion, Peebles remains skeptical of the neat "box in a box" that is our life in language, leveling these criticisms from within the most familiar of poetic structures. She gestures at the violence implicit in imposing an arbitrary structure on "real life," yet also the necessity of shared experience of language for creating a feminist consciousness.

Harryman, too, explores the relationship between language and gender, turning to invented and hybrid forms as a way of bridging the gap between tradition and innovation. Presented as a verse novel in discrete episodes, *Sue in Berlin* calls upon verse plays, lineated poetry, dramatic scripts, and the lyric essay to create a single narrative that is marked by provocative rupture and interruption. She writes in the opening lines of *Sue in Berlin*:

> From nowhere a distinguished looking
> Gentleman approaches our
> Band of withdrawn politcos
> He's dressed in a pale suit
> His extended hand
> Lit by the moon glows
> Whitely
> And Sue disappears

The collection begins with language that is accessible before pushing beyond tradition. The philosopher Paul Ricouer once distinguished between symbolic language, which is language that generates meaning, and the language of signification; here we are in the realm of signs, not yet in the work's richly imagined metaphorical terrain. This choice speaks to Harryman's carefully considered approach to experimentation, to entice the reader with what is familiar only to make them question every preconceived idea they may have about language, form, and what is possible within them.

In one of the book's final verse plays, "Anti-Masque," Harryman writes:

C2 (younger):	Heart in hand on wheel
	Head on
shoulder in window	
	Pale in winter
with slow time	
	Tree in
shadow by piano	
	Frequent a
stirring a template	
	Model for me
at breakfast...	

Her adherence to the conventions of grammar, syntax, and narrative early in the book open up a space for her to experiment boldly in the work's later passages. Here, the poetic line replaces the sentence as the primary unit of meaning, each enjambment marking the beginning of a new vocabulary of imagery, a new metaphor, a new logic governing the language that unfolds before us.

If a writer must, as Derrida argues, fight for respect after doing violence to literary tradition, these three gifted writers navigate this lingering conflict by stealing the very thing they had once wished to dismantle. By invoking the forms of a mostly male literary tradition, and summoning their implicit authority, they provocatively reframe a tradition that works to contain women's voices. Pragmatic and strategic, such an approach recognizes the necessity of a shared language and artistic repertoire, however fraught it may be, for creating a feminist consciousness. After all, it is the familiar structures of an inherited tradition that allow one to speak and be finally understood, to describe the contents of a room before burning it down.

THE VIOLENCE OF COLLISION:
NOTES ON COLLAGE, PRECARITY & THE ARCHIVE

In a co-authored essay, Priti Joshi and Susan Zieger observe that "Ephemerality might be described as the lived condition of an industrial modernity, founded on disposability, fluctuating value, and illusion." It could also be said that the fleeting nature of so much material culture challenges our beliefs about history, as it undermines pretensions to enduring cultural relevance. The archive, however, offers an exception to this rule, a space removed from capitalist frameworks, where the remnants of disparate historical milieu may collide, challenge, and illuminate one another.

Three recent collections of poetry and hybrid work explore the unique potentialities of the archive, a liminal space that is inevitably charged with tension and possibility. Kathleen Peirce's *Vault: A Poem*, Mary-Kim Arnold's *Litany for the Long Moment*, and Amy Pence's *[It] Incandescent* utilize collage, assemblage, and juxtaposition to explore the precarity of our beliefs about history, its narratives, and its structures. While vastly different in form and approach, these three texts share an investment creating dialogue across cultures and historical moments, but also, they expertly reveal the violence inherent in this collision. As Mary-Kim Arnold notes, "[t]he life is there, encased in its own death. Its own catastrophe."

For these three gifted and prescient writers, the violence inherent in collage, assemblage, and artistic collision is as inevitable as it is generative. Scholar and poet Myung Mi Kim has long noted the violence of the experiment, in which boundaries, traditions, and readerly expectations are destroyed in order to make way for something new. In *[It] Incandescent*, Amy Pence attributes this generative violence to history itself and the artistic legacy she herself has inherited. She leaves us with the image of Emily Dickinson, "collecting her horrors – a box inside."

*   *   *

Presented as a series of visual texts, Amy Pence's *[It] Incandescent* reads as an extended engagement with Emily Dickinson's poetry, one in which the adept placement of the words on the page heightens our experience of language. More often than not, we are unsure as readers whether to approach Pence's text as homage or destruction, a dismantling of tradition in order to create a bright aperture, that opening that beckons "through the sun-stilled trees."

In many ways, the destructive impulse inherent in Pence's poetics is ideally suited to the book's narrative arc. She explores, through fragmentation, ellipsis, and linguistic collage, the trauma housed within – and often buried inside – the archive, that "box of phantoms" that must, at some point, be opened. She writes, for example, midway through the collection:

> *It:* that Memory you have to step around, opon. *It,*
> unnamed and unpersoned, made the *It* in Emily go
> to her knees –
>
> At what cost our denial? How we go to our knees.

Pence creates a poetics of trauma and redemption, an aesthetic predicated on building narrative, and discovering meaning, "by degrees." In doing so, Pence shows us that as T.S. Eliot later argues, quite famously, the past is contained within the present. Here, history and modernity are conflated in even the texture of the language itself. By pairing words like "opon" with more colloquial speech, Pence shows us that history, its trauma, its silences, and its elisions are embedded within the minutia of syntax and grammar.

It is perhaps for this reason that collage and assemblage become a powerful form of resistance. It is the space between things that speaks most audibly, that gestures at the multitudes of what cannot, will not, be spoken aloud. "Above them, the Good Death / hovers," Pence writes, "that happen - / that   gap / before the slaughter." Here fragmentation offers a meditation of the precarity of voice, as the threat of not only silence, but also, self-censorship, looms large. Here the gaps, the ruptures, the elisions become performance, as Pence offers us language spectacularly aware of its own precarious labor.

*   *   *

For Arnold, as in Pence's work, the precariousness of voice and narrative are tangible, embodied, viscerally felt. Presented as a book-length hybrid text, which meditates on the narrator's adoption from rural Korea and subsequent search for her biological family, *Litany for the Long Moment* offers a poignant and beautifully crafted meditation on linguistic displacement. Arnold calls our attention – in prose as subtle as it is evocative – to the physical difficulty of inhabiting a language that is foreign to one's sensibilities. Indeed, she shows us the myriad ways that personal identity is predicated on place, and the precarity of this necessary context. "I remain tethered to abstractions," Arnold tells us, "mother, motherland, mother tongue."

As Arnold draws from the archival material surrounding her own childhood and family history, we are made to see – powerfully and indelibly – that the collision of languages, of cultures, of histories, often reveals their incommensurability. Arnold warns us, "Repeating a word loudly with more urgency will only get you so far." What is perhaps most powerful about this book, though, is the way Arnold gestures at language as an embodied phenomenon. "I am struck by….the apparatus of language," Arnold notes, "and the physical difficulty of making sounds that are unfamiliar." Throughout *Litany for the Long Moment*, the body seems to reject language that does not arise from its history, from the memories and narratives housed within its own walls.

Collage and assemblage offer a way performing and dramatizing this alienation, as well as revealing the violence of imposing narrative in a strange language. We are made to see – through the fragments of a story that cannot, will not, be spoken – there are some connections that narrative convention is ill-equipped to fully articulate. Arnold elaborates,

> Among the documents my mother kept are: several copies of a three-page "social study" of which I am the subject; a record of medical examinations, letters from the director of the orphanage where I lived for some time, and a few photographs of me: as a child in Korea, as I arrived in New York.

Here the aperture – that luminous space between "records" and "photographs" within the archive – becomes a performance, calling our attention to the artifice inherent in any narrative scaffolding we attempt to impose. Indeed, absence and elision seem more real, more true. Arnold shows us that some meaning can only be grasped in this precarious linguistic context, as there is always the thing for which there is no word, the word "you may not yet know you want to say."

*   *   *

Kathleen Peirce's *Vault: A Poem* continues this exploration of violence, the archive, and the unspeakable. Presented as an extended sequence, which takes the form of lineated verse, epigraphs, and lyric fragments, Peirce's work engages source texts dating from the Renaissance to the present moment, her poetry offering an interstitial space in which these disparate voices become a seamless chorus, gloriously unified in their lyricism. In many ways, Peirce's seamless integration of these many voices gestures at a kind of universality, the shared condition of being tethered to a language that does not fully do justice to inner experience.

In many ways, this gesture comes through most visibly in the moments between sections, where the reader is frequently asked to follow as we leap from one voice to another, one century to the next. Peirce reminds us that *after this* means *because of this*, yet at the same time, she approaches time as linear, recursive. As a result, our ideas about causation are destabilized through the work's provocative juxtapositions and associative leaps. She writes,

....Everything is broke.
Reddish feathers growing at the joint, the prolonged hand
remind, supply.

56.

swee swee swee the art, swee
the art, sweetheart

Here Peirce reveals the archive as a place where the rules of logic and causation no longer hold. As we transition from the surreal dreamscape filled with "broken" objects and "Reddish feathers," we find our predilection for narrative causation challenged and interrogated. Like Arnold and Pence, she shows us that this interstitial space of the archive offers a testing ground for new ways of imagining language, grammar, and the structures of meaning making. As in Arnold and Pence's work, there is violence inherent in this destruction of old models, but it is a kind of violence that makes even the most ordinary things "more wild, and more violet."

"THIS DESIRE FOR LINKAGE":
FORM, NARRATIVE & HISTORY IN RECENT POETRY BY WOMEN

More often than not, contemporary poets turn to lived experience for both inspiration and insight into the human condition. Although such writing can dazzle with its subtle yet sweeping realizations, an artist who takes this approach risks a final product that, no matter how painstakingly made, fails to extend meaning beyond the individual who created it. In four recent collections of poems by women, the authors risk and avoid this outcome with elegance and grace. April Bernard's *Romanticism*, Diann Blakely's *Cities of Flesh and the Dead*, Michelle Boisseau's *A Sunday in God-Years*, and Jesse Lee Kercheval's *Cinema Muto* skillfully situate personal narratives within a matrix of social and artistic upheavals. Although the histories recounted in these books range from regional to literary and even to theological, the four poets prove comparable in their enduring fascination with the past and its role in shaping their identities as modern female poets.

As these writers delve into the old photographs, silent films, and religious doctrines that have influenced the world they inhabit, their use of form proves striking. Bernard, Blakely, Boisseu, and Kercheval present their books as extended poem sequences, but each writer offers distinct stylistic variations. Taking the shape of couplets, hybrid prose, and lyric fragments, the histories recounted within the five collections have led each author to a fundamentally different literary self, which is revealed and enacted in the diverse styles of these four volumes.

In Diann Blakely's *Cities of Flesh and the Dead*, for instance, formal decisions compliment the author's meditation on identity and place, which remain inextricably linked throughout the collection. Written as a series of interconnected poems and smaller sequences, the book follows a middle-aged narrator as she travels from the

Tennessee of her girlhood to England, Manhattan, and Ireland, only to realize the indelibility of her southern upbringing. As Blakely renders these locales alongside home movies and Saturday matinees, the work itself functions as a collage of literary forms, ranging from sonnets to lyrics to free verse. This hybridity subtly complicates the narrator's attempts to identify herself fully with any of the various places that she inhabits, or, conversely, to dismiss selfhood as merely a product of one's origins. The tension that Blakely creates between form and content proves especially noteworthy in "Sewanee: 25th College Reunion, 2004":

> Those mills belching smoke in Yorkshire landscapes
> Would have starved without cheap Dixie cotton.
> An antique chest, earrings, some hand-cut glass--
> Freed by remains of a maternal dower,
> I joined the few girls allowed here, too smart
> Not to learn to surrender when amiss
> In history class, where home wars rarely bleed.

In this mostly untraditional sonnet, Blakely describes the speaker's attempt to embrace her Southern upbringing, an endeavor the poet undermines through a subtly executed volta, using the sonnet's prescribed form to qualify the character's acceptance of her own heritage. The poet presents this piece alongside lyrics and elegies for places to which the speaker does not feel such a profound connection. In creating this ambiguous portrait of the narrator's attachments and origins, Blakely complicates her speaker's narrative; this remains among the most compelling aspects of this volume of poems.

In many ways, Blakely's struggle with the American South and its checkered legacy is a uniquely female one, particularly since she uses the form of the poem sequence to juxtapose complex, and often conflicting, definitions of womanhood. Blakely continues to depict the problematic nature of the tangible, often disconcerting narratives in her poems through her use of collage. In "Back for the Wedding," the second poem in a series, she writes that,

Darlene herself had opened their front door
To Satan, felt rattlers' fangs sink righteously
Into her arm while messing with the cage,
Wanting to give Glen a new plaything for bed.
Darlene rarely slept there, gossips said:
Only one child, and him now turned sixteen.

Throughout this excerpt, the poet offers a bleak parody of church life in the South, but also its influence on how femininity has been constructed by those who reside there. By conflating Satan with the snake Darlene will use to charm her husband, Blakely suggests that womanliness remains inextricable from both traditional morals and the transgression of them. In this sense, "Back for the Wedding" evokes the dangers of embracing female identity within such a precarious framework. Significantly, the poet pairs this piece with "Suffer the Children," a poem that affirms the previous speaker's sense of injustice while simultaneously recognizing few alternatives to these received ideas about womanhood:

It's hard to be thankful
For greasy beans, harder to be a shepherd
When all you've got is goats on piss-poor land
Growing more rocks than wheat, those winter bucks
From ringing sales at Mr. Burns's store.

"Suffer the Children," as do many of Blakely's works, illuminates the poems with which it appears, in this instance through its speaker's recognition of the failings of traditional ideas about womanhood as well as the necessity of living in accord with them. Through adept sequencing, Blakely presents "Back for the Wedding" in an even darker light, one that reinforces the inescapability of the dangers and paradoxes it describes. Like much of Blakely's work, this poem uses juxtaposition to create fascinating contradictions and incongruities, an approach that often opens her poems to multiple readings.

While Blakely's use of hybridity and collage proves to be one of the book's strong points, *Cities of Flesh and the Dead* also creates a subtle sense of unity among its individual works through both form and content. Just as the various memories recounted within the collection are woven together by the narrator's constant return to her Southern heritage, iambic pentameter links the many poetic forms that appear over the course of the sequence. By creating this faint internal rhythm that carries through each piece, Blakely mirrors the narrator's constant awareness of her origins, deepening the irony and complexity of the moments in the book when she questions them. This trend proves especially apparent in a sequence called "Home Thoughts from Abroad," in which Blakely conflates familial origins with place. She writes in the second part,

> Rigid beneath blankets, I pray that they'll divorce
> Through years of long wall-trembling arguments.
> The night I tell my mother I'm engaged,
> She cries, of course, and offers me her ring.

Taking liberties with the sonnet form , this poem expresses its speaker's fear that she will, like her mother, find herself limited by the world into which she was born. Presented alongside poems in which the character longs "for blessing in [her] mother tongue" when abroad, the two individual works are gracefully linked by the steady iambic rhythm that carries through the sequence. Ultimately undermining the narrator's denial of her own origins through both form and content, the series, like much of the collection, proves to be as finely crafted as it is contemplative.

However, many of the book's disappointments go hand in hand with its triumphs. Although Blakely skillfully weaves together formal innovation, personal history, and sweeping observations on gender in the American South, the poems often fail to situate the narrator's experience as a white woman within the region's history of racial strife. Admittedly, such an endeavor would likely undermine the delicate sense of unity achieved by the book, as the poet would risk engaging too broad a subject to balance with this elegant harmony of form and content. Acknowledging the narrator's position as simultaneously privileged and oppressed, however, would allow the poems to serve as a point of entry to multiple, and often contradictory, visions of womanhood in the American South. Although not comprehensive in scope, *Cities of Flesh and the Dead* is filled with imaginative depictions of womanhood in which the speaker questions conventional ways of envisioning female beauty. In "The Triumphs of Style," Blakely writes that "Destruction's glamour, / Took the picture that caught my notice fastest." Such passages would be complicated in rewarding ways by treating the many vantage points from which ideas about femininity have been received and experienced in the South.

Nonetheless, it is still refreshing to encounter poetry that achieves a sense of coherence as a manuscript, yet continues to find beauty in the unresolved, often irresolvable, aspects of both Southern womanhood and the ways in which identity is shaped by place. In a series called "Blood Oranges," Blakely writes:

> I buy a bag, their scent acidly sweet
> Through waxed paper, sweet as envisioned love
> Made real. Why travel except this desire
> For linkage, even skewed; its fruits blessings
> We've dreamed foreign, their varied tastes received
> And welcomed as this blood orange leaking its sting
> Down my square, freckled, inherited chin?

As in other poems within the collection, Blakely portrays the self as simultaneously "inherited" and constructed by the life one leads. Like the speaker's "square, freckled . . . chin," the place into which one is born, as well as the histories that haunt it, remain inextricable from the self that one attempts to create. Throughout the book, this argument between destiny and choice is conveyed with an array of visually stunning images, suggesting the pain and splendor to be found within this struggle.

Like *Cities of Flesh and the Dead*, Michelle Boisseau's *A Sunday in God-Years* explores the mixed blessings of womanhood in the American South. Written as a series of interconnected poems and longer sequences, the collection alternates between the musings of contemporary female speakers and several found poems documenting the Boisseau family's slaveholding history. In doing so, the poet juxtaposes formalism with fragmentation, suggesting that experiences with pristine appearances often reveal themselves as vestiges of American culture's dark, complex history. In "Apologies," Boisseau's speaker contemplates the presence of oppression and social upheaval in her family's story, using quatrains to structure her poem.

> And me, grandchild who makes herself the hero
> since she's the teller of this tale. I writhe
> and what of it? How can I begin to recount
> the sins, a million ships on every ocean?

By presenting flawless four-line stanzas alongside a fragmentary will bequeathing slaves as property, Boisseau mirrors her narrator's process of discovery through style and sequencing. Just as the speaker's beliefs about her own identity and origins are challenged, Boisseau creates a sense of order through her use of traditional forms, a sentiment that she undermines with the disconcerting remnants of her ancestors' legacy.

In many ways, Boisseau's use of hybridity and collage proves similar to Blakely's juxtaposition of sonnets, lyrics, and free verse in *Cities of Flesh and the Dead*. Like her contemporary, Boisseau uses formal incongruities to illuminate her book's overarching narrative of self-discovery. Presented as a family album of sorts, which archives the memories and ephemera of several generations, *A Sunday in God-Years* works toward a more complete knowledge of this history, as well as the speaker's gradual coming to terms with it. In "A Sunday in God-Years," Boisseau describes the speaker's desire to unearth her own origins:

Up on the ancient hill the grand old house
they built is solitary now. . . .
As for me, a middle-aged white
woman, I didn't have to care
who'd notice me helping myself
to these grainy eons.

After this, the poet conveys the speaker's heightened awareness
of her own identity not through narrative, but by placing an
extensive family tree between poems. This visual embodiment
of the character's struggle with her ancestors subtly guides
the reader to the next phase of the sequence, in which the
speaker experiences a sense of resolution. In many ways,
the elaborately diagramed family tree achieves what a poem
could not at this stage in the sequence, particularly as it helps
the reader to experience the speaker's overwhelming grief
and distress as she is confronted with her family's legacy.

As the book unfolds, *A Sunday in God-Years* contemplates the
significance that these past atrocities hold for the speaker as a white
Southern female, situating the narrator as both oppressed and
oppressor in light of her family's history. At once plainly written
and endlessly thought provoking, Boisseau's poems continue to
explore this complex vision of womanhood through juxtapositions
of poetic forms. By revealing fragments of past inhumanities
within flawlessly executed couplets and sestets, the poet mirrors
the ways conventional definitions of femininity are complicated
by the narrator's family legacy. In a piece called "Outskirts of
Lynchburg," Boisseau elaborates, using quatrains to structure the
work.

In oak rings I keep
many secrets. Why talk
about them when
they're expressed
in the jerked, frayed

stem, in fruit not
of my own making.

Pairing this more stylized piece with a newspaper clipping written
by a freedman, entitled "Lost Brother," Boisseau's elegant sequencing speaks to the conflicts of identity experienced by many white
Southern women. The piece creates a sense of orderliness by using
four-line stanzas, then subtly undermines it with these fragmentary
texts, suggesting that the tendency to view women as an incontest-
ably oppressed class is complicated by these remnants of our culture's
history. This piece proves characteristic of Boisseau's work, particularly as the poet transcends personal and local history, allowing
individual characters to stand at the crossroads of far-reaching social
movements.

Although more overtly political than Blakely's book, *A Sunday in
God-Years*, like *Cities of Flesh and the Dead*, is at its best when allowing
past and present definitions of womanhood in the South to exist side
by side, and, even more importantly, to complicate one another in
thought-provoking ways. Blakely states, for instance, that "everything's inherited here," evoking the deterministic nature of female
identity in her speaker's community. As she and Boisseau delve
into the ways femininity has been defined by past generations of
Southerners, both poets skillfully juxtapose history with modernity,
suggesting that a contemporary woman's life is often lived within the
boundaries inscribed by those who came before her.

Boisseau's depictions of landscape often embody the tension between
old and new as it pertains to female experience. Invoking stunning
pastorals as a metaphor for the speaker's perceived connection to the
women of her family's past, Boisseau suggests that, as with the his-
tory-laden terrain that her characters inhabit, one's life is inevitably
built on a foundation laid by past generations, which she explains in
"Eighteenth Century Boisseau Farmhouse."
    A long glaring ladder meets, tweezers-like
    its crisp leaning shadow--the two long legs

of a huge being who's about to stride
over the fields and trees, over the excellent
fires made when old wood starts to burn.

In such passages, the poet suggests an affinity between the Boisseau
family history, particularly the way it has been etched into the earth,
and the speaker's inability to detach herself completely from this
difficult past. The character's challenging, often self-effacing process
of introspection becomes, in a sense, the destructive fire "made when
old wood starts to burn." As Boisseau draws these elegant parallels
between interior and exterior life, her identity as a Southern woman
becomes a source of both guilt and responsibility. For the speaker,
confronting the dark, complex history of the terrain she inhabits
offers a sense of resolution, or, in other words, the ability to reenter
this landscape from a different vantage point.

The few disappointing moments in Boisseau's collection occur
when the speaker of the poem expresses remorse for delving into
her challenging past, a task that the book reveals as both relevant
and necessary. Many of Boisseau's narrators question their ability to
understand family histories without self-aggrandizement, a rhetorical flourish that often undermines the author's compassionate
and thought-provoking treatments of race and gender. In "When I
Consider," the final poem of the collection, she writes:

> Big eye and little eye. Ego, ego.
> Consolation. A form of feeling. Sun-
> light ramps through the window. Hello, hello!
> I'm coming and coming every second,
> ninety-three million miles with my letters.

Unlike some of Boisseau's other poems that situate the speaker as
a constituent of her community's history, this poem honors the
speaker's retreat into interior monologue. Yet the most compelling
moments in the book are those in which the poet pursues this connection between individual experience and social upheaval. In such
works, Boisseau's characters consider the events of their lives, but rec-

ognize that looking beyond the self is a necessary part of introspection. By achieving these challenging, thought-provoking moments and then returning again to the speaker's individual identity, the poet undermines some of the most rewarding aspects of the collection. Nonetheless, it is easy to delight in poems that weave history with modernity, and use form in innovative ways to comment on the connection between the two.

April Bernard's *Romanticism* also explores the relevance that history holds for the present, addressing its questions through style as much as content. The past that Bernard delves into, however, proves to be a more artistic one; she uses conventional lyric forms--among them couplets and tercets--to question, and at times reenvision, the assumptions underlying Romanticism as an artistic movement. In "The Paper Goose," for example, Bernard invokes dramatic diction, parodying the melancholy associated with Romantic poets:

> The beast of my sorrow crumples and wads;
> it will not unfold into fluttering pennant, flowing
> water.
> Instead, all recalcitrant, it sinks as sorrow.

Here Bernard employs tercets to challenge how Romantics visualized the poet in society. As she gently mocks artistic trends of the past, her use of form suggests the relevance of outmoded aesthetic movements to contemporary writers. For Bernard, the poet's ability to express such "sorrow" remains rooted in the conventions of previous generations, which the poet ultimately reworks and revises.

Bernard depicts Romanticism as at once passé and ever-present in contemporary conceptions of beauty, femininity, and selfhood. For this poet, literature operates as a conversation in which writers respond to and contemporize past aesthetic trends. In her sequence, "The Heroine in the Novel," Bernard uses enjambment to illustrate this point:

> Hair-tossing was a habit, and ringlets
> pulled back under a blue straw bonnet. Oh, and that

laugh,
a merry laugh it was, and her eyes often
danced, I am afraid. But
she had a chin like a prize fighter.

Bernard parodies the tropes of Romantic fiction, particularly the
recurring presence of a beautiful yet defiant heroine in mass-mar-
keted novels. By placing line breaks before hackneyed descriptions
of this female character type, such as her "merry laugh" and her
"dancing" eyes, the poet creates subtle pauses that contribute to a
mocking tone. Much like the poem's pointed use of italics, Bernard's line breaks seem to suggest that Romanticism is a passé artistic
movement , but she skillfully undermines this sentiment as the poem
unfolds. By isolating the novel phrase "she had a chin like a prize
fighter," the author illustrates that these outdated conventions may
be wed with a more contemporary aesthetic, using enjambment to
heighten the reader's surprise at this juxtaposition.

For Bernard, understanding and responding to past ideas about
literature remain essential tasks. Much like *A Sunday in God-Years*
and *Cities of Flesh and the Dead*, *Romanticism* argues that surroundings
influence both identity and the capacity for self-expression. Bernard,
however, suggests that literary history remains inseparable from the
personal narratives that fill Boisseau's and Blakely's collections. Her
poem "Picture Postcard" exemplifies this trend:

<pext>Henry James is swimming under the Rialto
Bridge,
his corpus magically unharmed by the wash of the
chemical lagoon.
Byron, drunk on chocolate, sucks on Mary Shelley's
satin shoe
under a table at Florian's.
The pearly sky shrugs eternal shoulders and laughs,
or weeps, it is impossible to tell which.

In such passages, Bernard depicts literature and culture as, in many ways, inextricable. Just as the speaker finds herself unable to describe her surroundings without delving into the artistic legacies of James, Byron, and Shelley, the poet suggests that Romantic ideas remain embedded in everyday life. Bernard's use of couplets to structure her poem reinforces this connection between old and new. As she combines nineteenth-century literary allusions with a contemporary setting, she pairs an old form with a contemporary voice, suggesting that modernity remains merely a result of past intellectual traditions.

Bernard's writing is at its best when using form and technique to depict literary history in everyday life. In poems such as "Renunciation," "Pull the Water Lily," and "Straw Flowers," the poet situates modern experience within a history of artistic and philosophical upheavals, using three- and four-line stanzas to structure the poems. Like Blakely, Bernard uses form to suggest that poets live and create art within the boundaries established by previous generations, essentially inhabiting tradition. Bernard writes, for instance, in "Renunciation,"

> Since life is even more finely calibrated
> than a Henry James story, I find I must
> resolve to lose repeatedly
> yet not believe myself.

Here the speaker views personal experience through the lens of literary convention, suggesting that Victorian poems and novels have shaped modern experiences. By presenting the poem in faithfully executed tercets, Bernard reinforces her assertion that personal narratives, as well as the ways in which they are expressed, remain inextricable from past artistic tropes.

Bernard's book falls short only in those passages where the poet fails to recognize the relevance of the Romantic tradition to everyday life. Although for the most part a stunning collection, Bernard's use of parody to modernize and challenge Romanticism at times overshadows her efforts to illustrate its relevance. "The Oft-Wedded Waif" exemplifies this:

> While married to her third husband, a race-track
> tout, Clothilde opened a bakery.
> Cookies in the shape of babies and wolf cubs were her
> specialty.
> After her fourth and fifth husbands were apprehended
> by the authorities, Clothilde
> could be found weeping into the icing.
> The tear-dripped cookies secured her fortune.

Bernard's ironic depictions of "cookies in the shape of babies and wolf cubs" and "tear-dripped cookies" render Romanticism as an entirely outmoded artistic movement in which only humor may be found. While such passages occur rarely in the collection, they detract from Bernard's many insightful readings of Victorian texts and their relevance to modern life.

Nevertheless, *Romanticism* offers readers a graceful synthesis of literary history and traditional forms with a forward-looking aesthetic. Just as the speakers of her poems continually recognize the presence of Shelley, Byron, and Keats in contemporary life, Bernard demonstrates a refreshing awareness of her own artistic heritage. In the same manner that Blakely's female speakers "inherit" social conventions from the generations that came before them, Bernard recognizes the role of the past in shaping both identity and the parameters one of self-expression.

*   *   *

Jesse Lee Kercheval's *Cinema Muto* gives artistic traditions of the past a contemporary voice, offering readers a graceful synthesis of history and modernity. Written as a series of interconnected poems and smaller sequences, the collection recounts a journey to Le Giornate del Cinema Muto, the annual screening of silent films in Pordenone, Italy. As Kercheval's poems explore the social underpinnings of films such as I Due Sogni Ad Occhi Aperti, Ein Werktag, and Kohitsuji, she presents past art forms as necessary to understanding history, and hence crucial to understanding oneself. In the first poem of the collection, "Saving Silence," she writes:

> One hundred & fifty thousand
> silent films, eighty percent
> are lost to us
> as the dust our grand-
> parents returned to.
> So why do I care? Because
> my mother was deaf,
> because I am tired after years
> of talk-talk-talking.

Kercheval suggests an affinity between her knowledge of the arts and an understanding of family origins. Throughout the collection, these "one hundred & fifty thousand / silent films" offer a window into the world of "our grand- / parents" and the speaker's deaf mother, whose lives were shaped by their encounters with culture. As the book unfolds, social and artistic histories become inextricable from intensely personal ones, which prove necessary to understanding origins and identity.

Kercheval's pairing of experimental forms with historical subject
matter proves striking. Drawing from a variety of literary traditions, which encompass not only poetry but dramatic writing, fiction, and hybrid prose, *Cinema Muto* often enacts its statements about history, art, and culture through formal incongruities. Just as the speaker's identity proves inextricable from the cultural and artistic endeavors of previous generations, the poet's voice itself arises out of an assemblage of past literary traditions. She writes in "Fragments from Le Mogli e le Arance: Wives and Oranges,"

> "if not winter,
> then no pain   and there is
>   no winter here"

--the speaker: an old man (husband of the woman
with the little smiling dog?)

[Let me tell you how God made men and women
Oranges, it involved oranges.

Here, Kercheval presents Sapphic fragments alongside musings
on the spiritual undertones of this silent film. Pairing allusions to
classical poetry with stage directions, dialogue, and typography, the
poem melds a variety of literary traditions, ultimately drawing a
parallel between the cultural influence of such films and Kercheval's
distinctive voice. Just as in many of the poems within *Cinema Muto*,
the speaker's identity and ability to express herself arises from her
cultural and artistic inheritance, from her rich, but often complex,
literary heritage. Like many works in this collection, "Fragments
from Le Mogli e le Arance: Wives and Oranges" proves striking as it
enacts these assertions about art through subtle stylistic decisions.

Approached with these ideas in mind, the book's novelistic structure
lends itself to an extended exploration of art, history, and identity.
Written as a book-length sequence, the collection's use of recurring
characters and unchanging setting allows Kercheval to explore these
themes from a range of vantage points, all the while maintaining a
stunning sense of unity. As the sequence progresses, each poem in
Cinema Muto complicates the last, a quality that lends itself to multiple readings. In "Keeper of Light," for instance, Kercheval elaborates
on the connection she has established between artistic and personal
histories:

> I feel light streaming through me as if I
> were a single, bright frame of film & outside
> there is a calm like a great silent movie,
> like God were already sleeping,
> like I was   & I am.

By depicting the narrator as "a single, bright frame of film" in a
world that resembles "a great silent movie," Kercheval reinforces

many of the assertions about art and everyday life that she has made throughout the book. Just as Oscar Wilde famously argued that life imitates art, Kercheval suggests that imaginative feats like silent films often shape the values and practices of the cultures she inhabits. But because the narrator in "Keeper of Light" occupies such a liminal state of consciousness between sleep and wakefulness, the poet calls upon the reader to classify such observations as insightful, unreliable, or anything in between.

Likewise, Kercheval's decision to present her book in four acts blurs this distinction between everyday and imaginative life. Presented as both the story of a husband and wife attending Le Giornate del Cinema Muto and a silent film unto itself, the collection implements an ironic structure that lends itself to paradoxes and surprises. Like Kercheval's adept sequencing, this framing device compliments, and often complicates the individual works within the collection. She writes, for instance, in "This is not a silent movie--there is music,"

> Without knowing,
> I hunted for the liquid music that is you.
> Now, I hunger for the movement of your fingers,
> the pale almonds of your nails barely seen
> in dimness. In between each feature
> I pace the lobby   famished
> until the lights go down,

Kercheval establishes her speaker as occupying a different historical period than the art she consumes. By creating a framing device that allows this character to drift from one cultural moment to the next, the poet allows the reader to learn about silent film while also witnessing a process of interpretation and revision. For Kercheval, a work of art proves to be a moment of historical exchange in which individuals engage with the cultural artifacts that surround them in an effort to construct something new. By proffering her poems as one of the silent films that she interprets and deconstructs, Kercheval in the end extends an invitation to the reader to continue this ongoing process.

Although the book's novelistic structure and multiple framing devices at times strike the reader as a hermeneutic circle that could forever be interpreted and reinterpreted, *Cinema Muto* remains an impressive collection. At a moment when most poets are preoccupied with autobiography and interior life, Kercheval skillfully situates her own poems and her role as an artist within a broader cultural framework. *Cinema Muto* offers readers a synthesis of historical insights and formal innovation, a combination that proves provocative throughout.

All stunning in their own right, these four books reveal a renewed interest in both traditional poetic forms and the ways in which style can be used to explore historical subjects. For Diann Blakely, Michelle Boisseau, April Bernard, and Jesse Lee Kercheval, technique becomes a point of entry to thoughtful exploration of the past, especially its role in shaping contemporary poetic voice. These books offer a fascinating window into the enduring commitment to literary tradition in women's poetry.

"THE MEMORIES OF SO MANY RIVERS": HISTORY & THE PASTORAL IN RECENT POETRY BY WOMEN

In much of contemporary literature, one sees a renewed interest in family narratives, inherited traditions, and their ability to illuminate the present. While such books may captivate readers with sweeping realizations about the human condition, they often scrutinize personal insights at the expense of concrete description. With that said, five recent poetry collections by women resist this temptation with elegance and originality. Patricia Clark's She Walks into the Sea, Sharon *Doubiago's Love on the Streets*, Elizabeth Oness's *Fallibility*, Peggy Shumaker's *Gnawed Bones*, and Connie Wanek's *On Speaking Terms* use place as a point of entry to questions of selfhood and origin. As these poets consider the role of family in shaping female identity, their observations are carefully grounded in such diverse landscapes as the Sonoran desert, Appalachian valleys, and Midwestern grasslands.

The five collections prove to be as finely crafted as they are rich in tangible details. Although drawing from a variety of literary traditions, these poets consistently use form and style to complicate their descriptions of old photos, inherited possessions, and "summer leaves turning silver." In this respect, subtle technical decisions convey ideas not fully present in the texts themselves. Much like the books' lush pastorals, which seem to mirror and comment on the inner lives of their observers, their style allows multiple views of a given subject to exist within the same narrative space.

Throughout Elizabeth Oness's Fallibility, for instance, the poet's evocative landscapes and her technical feats serve complementary ends. Written in couplets, sestets, and tercets, the collection uses traditional forms to create startling juxtapositions, which suggest the contradictions inherent in the speaker's Irish-American heritage. As Oness presents "fairy invention" alongside "the blemished past," the terrain that her narrator inhabits serves as a locus for these conflicts of identity. The book opens with a poem entitled "Belleek," in which Oness writes,

> My grandmother cried leaving Ireland for the last
> time.
> I sat beside her on the plane
> staring down at the Cliffs of Moher,
> water breaking over the wrack-mired stone.
> She had shown me the house where she grew up,
> the nettled fields, the barn... (11)

For Oness, the Cliffs of Moher embody the two characters' shared heritage, as well as the vastly different generations that they inhabit. More specifically, this tension between family history and modern life is skillfully enacted in the structure of the piece. The first couplet suggests that the speaker and her grandmother may learn from one another, particularly as the younger character discovers the cultural heritage that she has been born into. By isolating the "wrack-mired" cliffs in the next stanza, Oness evokes the grandeur of multigenerational histories as the two individuals are dwarfed by the sweeping landscape. Although seeming idealistic, Oness elegantly undermines such an interpretation in the third couplet. Transitioning to "nettled fields," a house, and a barn unique to the grandmother's experience, the poet subtly suggests that aspects of one's cultural "inheritance" will never be fully accessible to her postmodern generation. Like many other poems in *Fallibility*, "Belleek" raises fascinating questions about personal origin through spectacular description and formal subtleties.

As the book unfolds, Oness uses similar strategies to explore the ways modern family life, much like the "wrack-mired" Cliffs of Moher in "Belleek," embodies both history and modernity. Through an elegant synthesis of form, narrative, and evocative pastorals, the poems in this collection suggest the difficulty of negotiating past with present. A poem called "Water that Feeds the Battenkill River" exemplifies this trend in *Fallibility*. In this piece, a youthful female speaker is confronted with the outmoded values of an older family member. Oness describes this girl and her father, who, like some parents of earlier generations, would have preferred a son,

> We had to be quiet; noise
> would scare the fish away.
> My line ran out, invisible in shade,
> bright where sun leaked through
> and touched it. In my hands
> the winding draw of the stream... (14)

Throughout this poem, the speaker presents herself as a paradox, a daughter playing the part of a dutiful male child by fishing with her father. Approached with these ideas in mind, many individual lines and stanzas evoke the hopelessness of her filling this familial role. Through a skillful implementation of caesura and enjambment, Oness presents impossibility after impossibility, pairing "quiet" with "noise," and ethereal "sun leaking through" the trees with "hands" that seem to hold onto it. With that said, the volatile images that fill the surrounding landscape (such as "the winding draw of the stream" and the darkness that seems to swallow the speaker's now "invisible" fishing line) suggest the instability of a family life rife with these sorts of contradictions. In general, *Fallibility* is at its best in moments like these, when readers observe form merging gracefully with content.

In many ways, Oness's discussion of family life arises from a uniquely female experience. As she depicts the narrators' discovery of her Irish-American heritage, the poet considers the ways women safeguard, rebel against, and reassess their ancestors' concepts of femininity. These passages are marked by the same careful use of form to complement, and often complicate, a given poem's content. "The Silver Screen" exemplifies this trend in *Fallibility*. In this piece, Oness presents grandmother, mother, and daughter side by side as they negotiate the competing definitions of womanhood present in Irish America. She writes,

> A portrait of my mother hung in the hall. She looked
> so perfectly finished.
> My mother buttons every button to the top.
> My grandmother's hand was mutilated: half a nubble
> thumb,
> two of her fingers shortened and skinny
> like chicken bones covered with skin.
> My mother wouldn't tell me how it got like that. (20-
> 21)

In this excerpt, Oness depicts the speaker's mother as embodying respectability and the desire for social mobility. In many ways, this character represents a traditional vision of femininity in her meticulous dress and blouse "buttoned to the top." Presented alongside a carousing, rebellious grandmother and a granddaughter who represents a more balanced perspective, Oness offers the full range of possible reactions to the gender politics that we inherit. Her subtle use of the couplet form complicates her message in surprising, often provocative, ways. The uniform, two-line stanzas used in the piece evoke propriety and order, yet Oness' occasional use of one-line and three-line stanzas skillfully undermine this apparent endorsement of tradition. Just as the granddaughter in the poem acknowledges these vestiges of the past while balancing them the present, the form of the poem allows tradition to coexist with an occasional divergence from it. Although Oness presents readers with this moderate perspective, her skillful use of anaphora (in which she repeats "my" at the beginning of nearly every line in the passage) suggests that the speaker undoubtedly acknowledges her origins.

In short, *Fallibility* is a stunning book, as well as a stylistically dazzling meditation on family life. The volume only falls short when Oness turns to sentimentality instead of the technical nuances that she proves capable of. Such poems are few and far between in this collection, yet detract from the book's sophisticated engagement with poetic form and pastoral writing. A piece entitled "March, West Virginia" exemplifies this tendency,

> Sitting in your kitchen, I know this
> could be my life. The mountains rise
> above the white-clotted valley,
> and here in the quiet, I mark this. (36)

By ending with a reference to the writing of the piece itself, such works seem heavy handed after reading "The Silver Screen" and "Belleek." Although the poem's sweeping mountain landscape proves stunning, Oness's style fails to complicate it in the same thought-provoking way as in many other passages in the book. Instead, "March, West Virginia" merely references itself, rather than leading into broader questions about the world. On the whole, though, the collection's strengths by far outweigh its shortcomings. Oness offers readers a stunning matching of form and content, which raises fascinating questions about family life and one's place within it. By using stylistic feats and evocative pastorals to comment on these poignant family narratives, Oness's book proves as multifaceted as it is finely crafted.

Connie Wanek's third book of poems, *On Speaking Terms*, also offers readers a thoughtful meditation on family history. Alternating between sweeping landscapes and domestic interiors, much of the work in this collection explores the ways we negotiate heritage and identity with other facets of our existence. As in *Fallibility*, Wanek's subtle stylistic decisions become a point of entry multiple, often contradictory readings of the text itself. In this respect, her uses of form and technique embody the highly individual, yet surprisingly universal, challenges encountered by her characters as they delve into the past.

Wanek's poems are at their best when images from the natural world, such as "old snow," "Isabella Lake," and a gust of wind, serve as a doorway to complex questions about the individual's place in contemporary family life. By using concrete things as loci for these intangible ideas about selfhood and modernity, the poems found in *On Speaking Terms* remain at once philosophical and carefully grounded. A piece called "Closest to the Sky" exemplifies these ideas. Wanek writes, describing the death of a loved one,

> Out the window an ancient spruce so near,
> little more than arm's length: I can see every needle,
> dull in the winter, sober green-gray,
> a peaceful color
> that never tries to cheer us falsely. (37)

Throughout this excerpt, the speaker looks out the window of a deceased family member's room, observing a "somber green-gray" pine tree that seems to embody her grief. Just as the narrator stands at the cusp of this desolate landscape, she similarly struggles to negotiate the challenges inherent family life, and eventually reenter the great outside world. In this respect, the dialectic between inner life and human interaction is gracefully mirrored as the poet transitions from domestic settings to sweeping pastorals. Much like the speaker finds shelter in memories evoked by her loved one's possessions, yet must return to her own difficult existence, the pine tree's dull needles simultaneously caution and beckon.

As the book unfolds, the structure of each individual poem complements these meaningful observations on family life and the natural world. Many of these works are written in two end-stopped stanzas, each of which reads as a poem unto itself. Just as the speakers found in Wanek's book project the absence of family members onto barren landscapes, the writings themselves are literally halved. A piece entitled "Rags" embodies this trend in *On Speaking Terms*. Wanek elaborates,

> Blue is gray not, like a patch
> of sky filthy with clouds.

> Why is piano dust always so gray?
> Something about sound waves
> and decay
> that science could explain.
> I didn't need a scissors
> the cotton was so rotted
> by sun and sweat, the salt I made... (23)

In describing this tattered piece of clothing worn by a loved one, the speaker find that it contains not only memories but the world as she sees it---"its sky filthy with clouds" and its "decay." Much like the grief-stricken narrator sees only desolation in her surroundings, and then in her herself, the poem itself is presented in two distinct parts. Although dividing inner and exterior life in such a way, Wanek depicts family life as permeating both aspects of one's existence. Just as the tattered cotton garment gracefully unifies both halves of this poem, which appears cut down its middle, the speaker's attachment to her loved ones carries through both her emotional life and her existence in the world. *On Speaking Terms* is filled with poems like this one, in which form and landscape serve as vehicles for thought-provoking discussions of family and identity.

With that said, the book's few disappointments go hand in hand with its triumphs. Although skillfully grounding each piece in tangible details of the natural world, Wanek at times focuses too closely on them. In these instances, the poet fails to find greater significance the "pine needles" and "pumpkins" that populate the collection, a quality that detracts from the book's unity as a meditation on family life. Such moments are few and far between, but are encapsulated in a piece entitled "Blue Ink." Wanek writes, cataloging associations called to mind by this commonplace item,

> You can conjure blue ink
> and write a check for more than you have.
> People will understand.
> Some days the lake is blue enough

to be bottled, or injected
directly into a pen,
though as the words dry
they disappear, letter by letter,
sparing you
serious embarrassment. (73)

Passages like this one prove remarkable in their inventiveness, particularly as the poet takes the reader from "blue lakes" to "bottles" and forged checks in describing this mundane object. Yet by ending the piece with the addressee's "spared embarrassment," and thus gesturing toward what could have been, the reader is left with nothing material to take away from this imaginative journey. The piece forms a stark contrast with works like "Rags" and "Closest to the Sky," in which everyday items serve as a point of entry to insights about the world as it is, as well as the ways it might have been. While Wanek's tendency to fixate on concrete things proves to be an asset in most instances, any virtue taken in excess risks distracting readers from nuances of style and description.

Like Oness' work in *Fallibility*, however, Wanek's poems prove stunning in their ability to transcend generations, rendering poignant family narratives as timeless as the landscapes upon which they are enacted. Some of the most affecting moments in *On Speaking Terms* focus on the narrator's attempts to move past the loss of parents and grandparents, eventually building a family of her own. With that said, Wanek elegantly juxtaposes elegies with love lyrics, evoking both loss and renewal. She writes in a piece entitled "Garlic,"

He's always in your bed;
he's never in your bed.
Garlic is or isn't in a dish
or sprouting
on the sunny windowsill,
an inch of green ambition

and a stirring
in the severed roots. (21)

Poems like this one prove striking as the speaker negotiates efforts
to forge a life of her own with her "severed roots." Moreover, by
allowing the clove of garlic to serve as a point of entry to these questions
about romance, sustenance, and personal history, Wanek suggests a
delicate balance between these disparate aspects of human existence.

Throughout *On Speaking Terms*, the poet's choice of form forces
these ideas into dialogue with one another, a theme that comes
across beautifully in a sequence called "A Parting." Wanek writes
in the voice of a mother speaking to her son, "We have to say
goodbye again so soon./Another seam torn open, another hole
in the pocket/discovered too late" (61). Evoking the sorrow
experienced as an older generation is eclipsed by their offspring,
Wanek's use of the poem sequence form allows multiple and
contradictory views of this phenomenon to exist side by side. She
writes, beginning the next section in the son's voice, "Don't worry,
I'll greet the wild goose for you,/the one you fed all summer/
in the reeds by the wide river" (61). Here Wanek implies that
the son's generation will prove responsible stewards of their rich
familial histories. Moreover, passages like this use subtle formal
decisions to suggest that, as in the scenic rivers and skies that
permeate the poem, the loss depicted in the first section comes
hand in hand with renewal. Much like this individual poem, *On
Speaking Terms* proves to be a wise and finely crafted collection.

Many of the poems in Patricia Clark's *She Walks into the Sea*
read as responses to these observations on family, grief, and the
natural world. Her stunning volume focuses on the unique bond
between mother and daughter, particularly its role in shaping
female identity. As she presents "the secrets of childhood"
alongside the challenges of adulthood, Clark allows lush pastorals
and formal nuances to mirror these ideas (8). In this respect,
She Walks into the Sea proves similar to *Fallibility* and *On Speaking*

Terms, yet at the same time remains closely focused on the significance that family histories hold for women in particular.

As Clark seamlessly blends elegy with pastoral, creating stunning landscapes haunted by memory, the structure of the book proves ideally suited to its subject. Presented as a book-length sequence, *She Walks into the Sea* offers readers a graceful progression from the grief experienced after a mother's passing to a sense of acceptance. Throughout the first few poems in the collection, for example, the speaker sees every shift in the natural world as a reminder of her own mortality, as well as that of her loved ones. By portraying "birdsong early mornings" and "newly opened leaves" as signs of time's fleeting nature, poems like "On the Air, Fragrant" and "Two Deaths" suggest that loss permeates every aspect of the speaker's surroundings, even as the terrain seems to renew and replenish itself (5). As the book progresses, however, the speaker of these poems begins to embrace temporality. Consider the following passage, taken from a piece entitled "Against Memorials,"

> There isn't one for the dame's rocket, its tall stalks
> reclusive in the woods, fading now but still
> scenting the path, or for the wood anemone, shy
> with its creamy white flowers, gone in a week.
> And I doubt you will hear one for the bleeding heart,
> two pink fringed ones I bought from Susan a full
> year now before her father's sudden death. (74)

Here Clark conflates the "sudden death" of a loved one with the cycles of the natural world. In many ways, her descriptions of the "dame's rocket" and the "wood anemone" suggest the superfluity of our attempts to mourn. For Clark, the splendor of the natural world is found in its ephemeral nature, which teaches the observer the significance of memory. Just as the piece alternates between spare couplets and lush three-line stanzas, in which the descriptive passages contained in the latter elucidate the wry observations found in the former, the poet suggests that memory illuminates nature's constant ebb and flow. In this respect, Clark uses form and visually arresting landscapes to situate personal loss within a broader trajectory of reflection and self-discovery.

As with Elizabeth Oness's *Fallibility*, Clark's engagement with the pastoral tradition offers readers a distinctly female perspective, which suits the book's subject perfectly. As she describes the speaker's journey from grief to acceptance after her mother's passing, Clark depicts the natural world as a refuge particularly well suited to the narrator's sorrow, as nature itself is the grandest of mothers. This theme comes across most notably in the first poem in the collection, "Hamadryad," in which Clark portrays the narrator as seeking not only "shelter" but a return to her most fundamental origins (3). She elaborates,

> ...When I seek shelter,
> I abandon it to the understory--
> calling myself hamadryad and also sorceress, water-
> and depth-seeker--counting the months till I can
> cut a branch for dowsing, divining-- (3)

This piece, like many others in the collection, adeptly uses enjambment to suggest that the speaker remains a constituent of the natural world, rather than merely an observer. As Clark describes the roles in which this narrator envisions herself, such as "hamadryad" and "sorceress," she includes the word "water" at the end of the line. By doing so, the poet suggests that the speaker not only perceives herself as interacting with the landscapes that she encounters, but rather, she remains a part of them.

In many ways, "Hamadryad" foreshadows Clark's use of landscapes to mirror and comment on the speaker's emotional life throughout the collection. By presenting the speaker as not only seeking nature's "understory," but also a "sorceress" who manipulates her surroundings, Clark subtly instructs the reader as to how the book should be read. Unlike Connie Wanek and Elizabeth Oness, who favor multiple possibilities for interpretation, Clark delineates a clear relationship between herself and the pastoral tradition, in which "leafs," "twigs," and "wind-bent pines" are continually mediated by the speaker's emotions (30). This clarity of authorial intent proves to be one of the great strengths of the collection. She write in "Summer Canticle,"

> It comes to matter, in the yard, that the western bed
> flourishes with native plants, that Solomon's seal,
> tall bellflower, and garden loostrife, gold, return
> on their own. They follow the lately departed
> without
> mourning or lament, the pale creamy peony that
> nodded off... (28)

Although passages such as this one could be interpreted in multiple ways, "Hamadryad" offers valuable guidance as to this individual poem's place in the collection. Instead of approaching this excerpt as a meditation on nature's simplicity when compared with human existence, the opening piece suggests that "Summer Canticle" actually shunts such a reductive approach. For Clark, these "tall bellflowers" and "pale creamy peonies" offer insight as to the ways social practices, particularly those surrounding mourning and grief, have diverged from the natural world. The narrator's realization of this phenomenon is skillfully projected onto the garden that she inhabits. In this respect, Clark allows the individual works found within the book to illuminate one another. *She Walks into the Sea* proves stunning in both its coherence as a full-length manuscript and its complexity.

Approached with these ideas in mind, readers will find no difficulty overlooking the book's minor shortcomings. Clark continually searches for the "understory" of the landscapes she inhabits, but this profound understanding of nature at times overshadows her compelling observations on family. In such poems as "Thin Places" and "Late Photo of My Mother," she reveals some of the memories that haunt the stunning vistas that her narrator inhabits, yet one observes that such pieces do offer a complete picture of the character's family life. Some might argue that with a better understanding of the speaker's grief, readers would be fully equipped to appreciate Clark's remarkable ability to project these difficult emotions onto landscapes. *She Walks into the Sea* nevertheless offers readers a thoughtful meditation on loss and the natural world. Carefully structured and deliberate in its stylistic decisions, this book proves to be a distinctive variation on the similar projects of Connie Wanek and Elizabeth Oness.

Peggy Shumaker's *Gnawed Bones* also offers readers a graceful synthesis of elegy and pastoral. Much like *On Speaking Terms* and *She Walks into the Sea*, this stunning collection attempts to situate the loss of a family member within the ebb and flow of the natural world. In doing so, Shumaker draws fascinating parallels between her own self-expression and the sweeping landscapes that she describes. Much like the work of a poet, nature is revealed as an ongoing process of creation, which just as often involves destruction. In this respect, *Gnawed Bones* reads as a multifaceted, yet carefully executed, meditation on personal loss.

As the collection unfolds, Shumaker's formal range proves striking. Frequently juxtaposing couplets and tercets with fragmented texts, the book's style subtly mirrors the speaker's vision of her surroundings as "the first world/and the last" (13). "Beyond Words, this Language" and "Radio Control" exemplify this trend in Shumaker's writing. She writes in the first,

> The morning you died
> > I held your hand.
> What's left
> > to forgive? (48)

Shumaker's use of fragmentation subtly enacts the ways the speaker's family life has been distilled to its essence in the face of tragedy. Just as there's nothing "left/to forgive" of the elusive father figure in the poem, the piece itself appears as the few necessary words among many possible narratives. Contemplative and thought-provoking, Shumaker's book transitions from this elegy to a more hopeful piece entitled "Radio Control," which depicts a pilot's first flight. What's more, this movement from destruction to transcendence is skillfully mirrored in the poet's shift from lyric fragments to orderly, pristine quatrains. Just as the "Radio Control" suggests that hope and possibility will eventually be restored to the speaker's life, the poem itself enacts this return to the natural order of things. Shumaker elaborates,

> After that,
> while your daughter choked
> on words she'd scrawled
> to honor you, above us all
>
> came the whining hum
> your craft out of sight
> wing and roar
> sailing over. (49-50)

Although "Radio Control" proves compelling as an individual poem, Shumaker's juxtaposition complicate it in thought-provoking ways. In many respects, the transcendent tone of the poem reads as commentary on "Beyond Words, this Language" and its mournful subject. Shumaker suggests through these pairings that the speaker will overcome her grief and loss, much like a natural order is restored to the poem itself as she transitions from fragmentation to formalism.

With that said, Shumaker's poems lend themselves to multiple and often complex readings, in which observations on the writing process exist alongside poignant family narratives. Throughout *Gnawed Bones*, the two disparate subjects are gracefully woven together by the poet's fascination with the nature and its ongoing processes of both creation and destruction. In the title poem of the collection, for instance, Shumaker gracefully merges elegy with a thoughtful meditation on self expression, both of which she envisions as part of the cycles of the natural world. Just as births and deaths remain part of the incontestable order of things, the act of paring a poem to a few truly essential words involves the same processes of invention and eradication. She explains in "Gnawed Bones,"

> If every day
> re-enacts creation,
> if we live
> here, now
> in the first world
> and the last,
> let us speak
> in our bones
> languages of water
> from all skies, from
> deep underground. (13)

In many ways, works like "Gnawed Bones" posit the natural world as our most fundamental origin, the source of literary invention as well as personal loss. For Shumaker, then, desolate landscapes and sweeping vistas serve as a point of entry to the full range of human experiences, which in turn give way to artistic expression. In this respect, *Gnawed Bones* proves comparable to Patricia Clark's *She Walks into the Sea*, which presents nature similarly in such poems as "Hamadryad" and "Summer Canticle." Although analogous in this sense, *Gnawed Bones* is distinguished by its attempts to situate even everyday speech within the harmonious ebb and flow of the natural world.

In many respects, this ongoing fascination proves to be one of the great strengths of the collection. As the book progresses, Shumaker explores the ways in which nature's tragedies and triumphs are enacted in language, revealing any given word as embodying such beauty and ferocity. In a prose piece entitled "Dive," for instance, a single word becomes a point of entry to questions of artistic invention, personal losses, and the ability of the human spirit to survive them. Presented as three distinct attempts to define this ambiguous term, the piece begins by describing the exploration of a reef,

> Its prized almost to extinction, its numbers spiraling down, down. And so the crown-of-thorns star munches in a few weeks corals that take decades to grow, corals that shelter nurseries for damselfish, angels, eels, the small fry the rest of the world depends on. In their wake, hungry stars leave acres of skeletons, bleached. (24)

Passages like this one suggest that the natural world and the equilibrium that enables it to sustain life remains precarious. By opening the poem in such a way, the poet draws a comparison between "the crown-of-thorns star" endangering the balance of nature and the ways that personal tragedies disturb what once were harmonious lives. She writes in the third piece in the sequence,

> I bring home a sturdy walker that fits him, complete with a seat he can sink into when he tires. We store the rickety frame his wife Suzie pushed for two decades, through not knowing, through lupus, through ovarian cancer, through knowing. Tonight its synchronized events, athletes perfectly attuned, years of daily practice peaking, if they're lucky, into two forms/one motion. (25)

In many ways, this excerpt suggests an affinity between nature's ability to both sustain and destroy itself and the unexpected hardships that family life brings. As Shumaker delves into these difficult subjects, the form of the poem proves reminiscent of a dictionary entry, which suits the subject perfectly. Much like the precarious equilibrium supported by the reef in the first section and the caretaker in the third, the word "dive" itself is made to bear the weight of all these tragedies and triumphs. A poem as subtle as it is finely crafted, "Dive" suggests the ways in which language supports a delicate balance between its own beauty and its intensity.

On the whole, Peggy Shumaker's *Gnawed Bones* is remarkable collection. Ambitious and contemplative, the book skillfully negotiates stylistic nuance with larger philosophical questions. *Gnawed Bones* represents a beautiful synthesis between form and content, as well types of subjects. As Shumaker transitions from nature to personal tragedy, her ability to weave dissimilar subjects and put them in dialogue with one another proves striking.

Sharon Doubiago's *Love on the Streets: Selected and New Poems* also elaborates on this perceived connection between familial history and the natural world. In many ways, her work presents family ties and the places that represent them as political, for they often represent provocative questions about gender and nationality. As Doubiago's poems transition from the Washington coast to Long Beach and eventually South America, she seeks to transcend the boundaries that we tend to delineate between social groups. For Doubiago, the unconditional regard that family members have for one another serves as an ideal for the society that we inhabit. As she explores the possibility of a better world, this gifted poet shows that the terrain we occupy, much like the human spirit, remains too resilient to be divided by beliefs about ethnicity, gender, and nationality.

With that said, Doubiago's syntax compliments her subject matter in thought provoking ways. Frequently invoking repetition and anaphora, the poems in this stunning collection mimic the style of such classical texts as Ovid's *Metamorphoses* and Sophocles' *Oedipus Rex*. In this respect, Doubiago's work resembles that of Elizabeth Oness, who also uses technique to situate her speakers within a complex cultural tradition. Moreover, as Doubiago places her narrator's family life within a broad trajectory of artistic upheavals, she skillfully suggests the ways that these bonds are shaped by a range of societal influences. A piece entitled "Father," which describes a young girl fishing, provides some insight into this aspect of *Love on the Streets*. Doubiago writes,

> I am like you, Mama always said.
> Often we went fishing.
> It takes patience and silence
> to be a fisherman.
> Most fail, you always said.
> I am like you, Mama always said,
> and if I reach back far enough
> we are fishing again from the narrow rock ledge... (7)

By repeating the phrase "I am like you" at the beginning of each stanza, as well phrases like "you always said," Doubiago creates a stately tone, if effect gesturing toward a complex, international literary tradition. These stylistic nuances create a stark contrast with the poem's childhood subject matter, yet this tension proves to be the great strengths of works like "Father." For Doubiago, these sorts of cultural influences permeate even the most naive moments of a child's life, in this case the speaker's emulation of her father and his knack for fishing. Just as the style of the poem evokes this very idea, Doubiago's visually arresting imagery weaves together the people, places, and disparate narratives that have shaped this speaker's identity.

For Doubiago, the landscapes that her speakers inhabit evoke similar questions about history, family, and the self. As *Love on the Streets* unfolds, she suggests the ways in which society has degraded both individual identity and the stunning vistas that surround us. In this respect, Doubiago's thought-provoking work posits modern existence as constructed and artificial, rather than instinctual, as family life is portrayed throughout the collection. A piece entitled "Signal Hill" exemplifies this tendency in the collection. The poet writes, describing her father's visit to a bar on the way home from work,

We come here every Friday when he gets paid
but my brother and sister are still afraid
of the creatures nodding in the dark
we are parked between.
The city spreads beneath us
in a rainbow-spilled oil puddle. (3)

The speaker of the poem, although unconditional in her love for her father, observes the ways in which contemporary gender roles have corroded familial relations. Although the man in the piece longs to escape his responsibilities, the narrator suggests that the obligations of providing for others will still await his return. Much like the "rainbow-spilled" landscape that has been polluted by society, the speaker of the poem suggests the ways in which social categories have dictated our concepts of selfhood and identity.

As Doubiago offers these astute social criticisms, she frequently returns to the family as a structure in which individuality is embraced, as opposed to stifled. Moreover, Doubiago presents the speaker's enduring affection for her brothers, sisters, and parents as innate, much like her appreciation of the stunning coastal vistas that populate the collection. A sequence entitled "Psyche Drives the Coast" exemplifies this trend in *Love on the Streets*. Doubiago writes in the second section of the piece, entitled "'It don't mean a thing if it ain't got that swing,'"

He asks her
to marry him, saying *the deep
anguish in your eyes
speaks pages
of dialogue*. But it grows
dark. Fishing lights bob the way out.
Her husbands signaling her, who might
know her. One more tune at their windows, she lets
go
a girl crying in their arms. Then leaves

her face behind. Goes back out.
The sea loud. (49)

In this passage, the speaker prepares for marriage and a family life of her own. As the piece unfolds, this narrative merges gracefully with a description of the coastal landscape she inhabits, ultimately suggesting a connection between familial bonds and the natural order of things. Just as the speaker is simultaneously beckoned by her "husbands" and the vast ocean itself, Doubiago presents family relations as one of the most fundamental aspects of life on this on this earth.

As Doubiago seeks to extend this sort of unconditional regard to not just our own families, but to all living things, her use of found language fragments proves striking. Just as the poet suggests that different social groups may coexist, the poems themselves force dissimilar types of speech into dialogue with one another. In many ways, Doubiago's use of fragmentation to mirror her subject matter resembles works like "Beyond Words, This Language" in Peggy Shumaker's *Gnawed Bones*, yet at the same time proves to be more overtly political. A piece entitled "Hip Hop Hopi Hope" exemplifies this tendency in *Love on the Streets*. Doubiago elaborates,

> Gypsy is from Egypt
> which is really Greek and pronounced
> *hee hip*. Hee hip son. He and her and their son. Ho!
> Hippie
> is a Sioux word
> meaning "he is there, she is here, they are everywhere"
> holy, happy, homo, hepcat, hipster, hippie, homey,
> helpless, homeless ho
> hippity hop, hopilong bebop and hop scotch to (135)

By presenting words like "bebop" and "hopscotch" alongside ancient Greek, the poem subtly mirrors the world that it describes. Just as Doubiago suggests that people should embrace the individuality of those around them, the piece itself culls words from a variety of nations and social groups, illustrating the ways they may illuminate and complement one another. Moreover, as the narrator of the book traverses diverse terrains, seeing them all as interconnected, individual works like "Hip Hop Hopi Hope" suggest that social relations should be approached with these same ideas in mind.

All points considered, Patricia Clark's *She Walks into the Sea*, Sharon Doubiago's *Love on the Streets*, Elizabeth Oness's *Fallibility*, Peggy Shumaker's *Gnawed Bones*, and Connie Wanek's *On Speaking Terms* provide a fascinating window into the emerging interest in family history and the pastoral in contemporary women's poetry. Each stunning in its own right, the five collections showcase a growing concern with personal origin in recent writing, which has given way to tense and thought-provoking relationships between style and content.

"MY HEART WAS CLEAN":
ON THE WORK OF SILENCE IN POETRY

IN *THE METAPHYSICS OF YOUTH*, WALTER BENJAMIN observes that "[c]onversation strives toward silence, and the listener is really the silent partner. The speaker receives meaning from him; the silent one is the unappropriated source of meaning." In other words, it is the space between words that sets off language, the dim background against which a light becomes visible. For Benjamin, silence was the precondition for a community out of which story arises, and the vast expanse waiting just beyond its inevitable end.

Three recent collections of poetry fully do justice to this complex relationship between silence, narrative, and the tacit relationships out of which language is borne. Julie Marie Wade's *When I Was Straight*, Eileen G'Sell's *Life After Rugby*, and Rajiv Mohabir's *The Taxidermist's Cut* each consider, albeit from vastly different conceptual vantage points, the ways silence makes possible our experience of beauty, that "gift of dark lace" woven into each poem in these finely crafted collections. For G'Sell, Mojabir, and Wade, the possibility of transcendence resides in the space between things, and it is always a bright aperture that gives rise to a "queer flutter that knocks about your ribs." Though vastly different in style and sensibility, these three books share an investment in allowing opulence to be complimented by the reader's own unspoken imaginative work and contemplation, offering us only "the sound of boots through snow and the dark."

What's more, these writers show us a full range of approaches to the work that silence can do. In G'Sell's dense, image-driven lyrics, this purposeful withholding often takes the form of absent narrative scaffolding. "Arias" and "attics" exist in close proximity, yet we are never told how these relationships came to be. What is left unsaid becomes an invitation to the reader, a pathway into the book's rich fictive terrain. For Mohabir and Wade, however, each aperture manifests as a kind of rupture, a subtle violence done to voice and language. As Mohabir himself tells us, "Every time you speak they hear a different hell."

*   *   *

In *Life After Rugby*, each line is gratifyingly dense in its presentation of images, types of rhetoric, and its vibrant soundscapes. For G'Sell, this disconcerting proximity - of images, of lexicons, and of narratives - gives rise to countless elisions, as the relationships, the rules that govern this imaginative topography, are often left to the reader's imagination. Indeed, we are offered "a cheekbone shyly brushing your wrist," though the speakers of these poems rarely tell us to whom a body, or an encounter, belongs.

In many ways, silence is intricately linked to pacing in this work, as the speed with which we transition does not afford time or space for exposition. It is the breathlessness of each poem, their restless movement and their dense, complex music, that allows silence to inhabit them so fully. After all, the relationships, the associations, and the resonances, are too numerous to count. Reminiscent of Joshua Clover's *The Totality for Kids* and Kathleen Peirce's *The Ardors*, G'Sell's poems also fearlessly confront --- through their satisfyingly dense constructions and their quick, unpredictable leaps --- our own discomfort with silence, while at the same time, gesturing at its inevitability. G'Sell elaborates,

> With the best of her Sugar Ray Leonard bob,
> She weaved beyond traffic.
>
> Symphony, prosperity, the loose mares of time.
> Homily of hominy, the long dreams and lime.
> Outside her glowing loungecar, igloos in space.

In many ways, these lines might be read as an ars poetic, as G'Sell gestures as the work's own "symphony" of disparate images, lexicons, and miniature soundscapes. In passages like this one, the reader begins to see that the poems are constructed against silence – as the speaker fills the air with her "Sugar Ray Leonard" and nonsensical rhymes – but also, that the poems exist because of that negative space, as it is the absence of narrative scaffolding, and all that is left unsaid, that allows the story to grow wilder.

*   *   *

Mohabir's poetry reads as a novel variation on G'Sell's exploration of silence, elision, and readerly unease. While formally diverse, spanning tercets, couplets, and hybrid experiments, *The Taxidermist's Cut* is gracefully unified by an exploration of silence as a kind of violence, a rupture in the faultlessly woven tapestry of voice, narrative, and community. Mohabir writes, "Knowledge / of Violence: // where welts rose on my legs / from the riding crop hidden / by your headboard / the crumble of song / shuddered in my hands." Here lineation, and its ensuing pauses, exist in tension with the sentence, as well as the syntactic unit. Clauses (like "knowledge of violence" and "hidden by your headboard") are halved by Mohabir's deft and provocative lineation. When read through the lens of the book's exploration of cultural otherness, these stylistic gestures take on a new and conceptually arresting significance, as Mohabir shows us that silence – in poetry, in culture, and in our own consciousness – is politically charged.

Through his accomplished craft and thoughtful approach to style, Mohabir shows us the myriad ways that censorship, and that fear, deeply rooted in our culture, of confronting difficult questions – is gradually internalized, shaping one's conscious experience even in solitude. This, Mohabir shows us, is the ultimate form of violence and intrusion. He elaborates,

> Your parents are at Bible study, leaving you alone
> with the devil inside. Your clothes are strewn about
> the floor.

The rain richochets drops through
the windowpane.

Your drops drone and soar form the opened window
as cicadas.

Inside you rain. You are a forgery. Not a wolf. Not
an Indian. Not a son.

What is particularly revealing in this passage is Mohabir's adept
and skillful use of caesura. Here, the work's meaningfully timed
pauses, the persistent stop and start, give rise to an uneasy, hesitant
music (most visible in phrases like "…as cicadas. Inside you
rain."). We are shown that the voice of culture (which manifests
powerfully in lines like "You are a forgery") ultimately engenders
silence, even in the speaker's uncontested solitude. Yet at the same
time, Mohabir calls our attention to the music that silence allows
us to hear. What's more, he reminds us of the persistence of voice,
and of music, even as the voice of the establishment "drones"
through "the opened window."

*   *   *

Like Mohabir and G'Sell, Wade's poetry exists at the interstices of
speech, silence and unease. Presented as a book-length exploration
of the speaker's life before she came out as a lesbian, the poems in
this stunning collection are haunted by a kind of shadow story,
a narrative that resides just beneath the surface of these lively,
jocular poems. Like G'Sell's poetry, these pieces exist against
silence, and the confrontation – with selfhood, identity, and desire
– that inevitably ensues.

As the book unfolds, each poem becomes a poignant dramatization
of what's left unsaid. Yet at the same time, speech calls attention to
its own artifice, as Wade's poems are constantly gesturing– at turns
playfully, knowingly, and sorrowfully – toward all that cannot,
will not, be spoken aloud. "I could tell my mother how / I wanted

her to brush my hair / & braid it with ribbons, Wade writes, "I could tell my father how / I loved baking cookies & / pinning damp clothes on the line." Here what's perhaps most revealing is the line break and ensuing pause before "pinning damp clothes on the line." The moments of elision, as in Mojabir's work, becomes politically charged, as Wade's speaker struggles to signify and perform an identity that is foreign to her. Through her silence, the speaker also experiences herself as foreign, and this, for Wade, becomes the ultimate form of violence.

Yet she also shows us silence as agency, as manipulation of a cultural system, as well as readerly expectations. "I might have smiled more then," Wade writes, "the part of my lips so often mistaken / for happiness. In fact, it was something else--- / a fissure, a break in the line---the way / a paragraph will sometimes falter / until you recognize its promise as / a poem." In much the same way that Wade's speaker masquerades in her interactions with others, the moments of rupture and elision within the poem ultimately toy with the reader's preconceived ideas about how a narrative should or ought to unfold. Here the pause, that subtle and playful rupture before "a poem," the subsequent delay before narrative resolution, exemplifies the ways silence in Wade's work gives rise to suspense, surprise and wonder.

Indeed, that speechlessness engendered by culture is appropriated, and recontexualized in a way that empowers the speaker, rather than censoring her. Like Mohabir and G'Sell, Wade shows us that each moment of elision contains multitudes within it. It is in these liminal spaces – the glowing aperture, the tentative sigh, the pause for breath - that the rules of language no longer hold, and anything becomes possible.

"SPARE THIS BODY, SET FIRE TO ANOTHER": SPEECH & SILENCE IN WORK BY KAVEH AKBAR, BRENNA WOMER, & HENK ROSSOUW

IN THE ONE VOLUME OF WRITING that he published during his lifetime, Ludwig Wittgenstein claimed that "the limits of my language are the limits of my world." Indeed, grammar, and the rules that govern speech acts, inevitably structure our relationships, determining what can – and what may never – be said between two people. Even in solitude, it is linguistic convention that circumscribes the boundaries of our dreaming, even as we begin to sense that bright expanse that lies just beyond our reach.

Three recent poetry collections skillfully interrogate the limitations of language, exploring ways that we as readers and creative practitioners can expand the boundaries of what is communicable, giving voice to all that is "wilding around us." Kaveh Akbar's *Calling a Wolf a Wolf*, Brenna Womer's *Atypical Cells of Undermined Significance*, and Henk Rossouw's *Xamissa* share a commitment to making audible that which lies at the outermost periphery of language. Though wide ranging in style and conceptual approach, these three gifted writers turn to experimental forms as a means of critiquing of linguistic convention, calling attention to its arbitrary limitations. Indeed, theirs is a critique that performs and dramatizes its grievances with respect to grammar, and we watch as that "whole paradisal bouquet spins apart."

What is perhaps most striking about these writers' experimentation is the way their gorgeously fractured forms invite silence into the work. As each of these three collections unfolds, we watch as moments of rupture, elision and interruption gesture at all that lies beyond the printed page. Akbar, Wommer, and Rossouw show us that "we are forever folding into the night," and they give us, through their bold experimentation, a vocabulary for articulating its "regret," "its spiritual conditions," and "its diamonds."

Akbar's *Calling a Wolf a Wolf* is structured as a series of linked persona-driven pieces, many of which make expert use of white space within the line. As the book unfolds, these seemingly small gaps within the text proper accrue vast, wide-ranging, and unwieldly emotional resonances. "As long as earth continues / its stony breathing, I will breathe," the speaker tells us. And in much the same way that Akbar makes us attend to the almost imperceptible rhythms of the physical body, he calls our attention to the space between words, suggesting that the very foundation – of meaning, of speech, of communication – resides there.

When we first encounter silence in the work, it is in the first moments of the opening piece, "Wild Pear Tree." Here, the poetic line is literally halved, a gap manifesting in the very center, its form making visible all that is yet unspeakable: "Its been January for months in both directions   frost..." What's perhaps most revealing about this passage is Akbar's use of white space to amplify the limitations of the language we do encounter. Here, we sense a sorrow just beyond the pristine imagery that we are actually given. It is that sorrow that cannot yet be named, that finds a name over the course of the book-length sequence. In these opening lines, however, all that is at that moment unspeakable – addiction, longing, excess and its disappointments – is rendered as a startling absence, and that elision is what gives rise to the wonderfully imperfect and awe-stricken music of these poems.

Silence becomes the driving force of the work, the language merely orbiting around its alluringly absent center. Akbar writes, for example,

> they all feel it   afterwards the others dream
>
> of rain their pupils boil the light black candles
>   and pray the only prayer they know
> *oh lord*
> *spare this body*   *set fire to another*

Here Akbar invokes silence as a way of performing and dramatizing time, both literal time and lyric time, that temporality which is measured in emotional, visceral, and psychic duration. It is the sense that time has elapsed ("they all feel it afterwards") that changes our encounter with the words that do exist on the printed page. But also, it is this sense of time passing that signals all that has been elided by the narrative itself. Here past and present are juxtaposed, and it is the reader's task to create the lovely narrative arc that lends meaning, unity and form to experience. By gesturing at the arbitrary nature of language, narrative, and their repertoire of forms, Akbar opens up the possibility of alternative models for structuring lived experience. And by the final lines of the poem, we are given one in the deus ex machine that inhabits the final line: *"spare this body set fire to another."*

If narrative is a kind of conjuring, an appeal for meaning, structure or order that may not be immediately apparent, language is the space in which that alterity makes itself known. The meaning that we arrive at through the unwieldly apparatus of grammar is indeed an otherness, a specter that haunts a room that is not its own. What's more, it is the space between words where the ghosts of "corpses" and "chariots," the "blank easels" and "orchids" of memory, actually live, waiting for a body to breathe into.

*   *   *

Like Akbar's *Calling a Wolf a Wolf,* Womer's *Atypical Cells of Undetermined Significance* explores the ways in which silence, rupture, and elision call into question all that resides on the printed page. She takes physical illness and medical trauma as her subject, interrogating the body as a discursive construction, knowable only through our relationship to language. In much the same way that Akbar forces the reader to attend to the space that separates words, and the almost imperceptible rhythms of the human body, Womer calls our attention to the transitions between the many discrete episodes that comprise the book. For Womer, the female body resides in these apertures, in that bright and liminal place between the various narratives and myths that have been imposed from without.

Presented as an extended sequence of hybrid texts, which shift rapidly between "psychic injury," "emotional shock," and "Lipton iced tea powder mix," Womer's writing mirrors the experience of being a patient through the behavior of its language. She actively involves the reader in the struggle to glean meaning in the space between fractured, contradictory, and ultimately incommensurable fragments of text. Womer writes, for example, in "When a Psychic Says We're Soul Mates,"

> Recall how you know the heart,
> and remember the future, the
> brain, the chronic hunger and
> burn; life in a wet summer, loud
> and close---eternal, intolerable.
>
> Number the young.

After this lyrical meditation on the delights and displeasures of the human body, Womer transitions to a prose vignette:

> We drove in the day before Hurricane Isabel with our
> lives blocking the rear view of our Ford Expedition.
> There was no available housing...

In the moment between sections, that brief pause, the body shifts from being a site of pleasure (and emotional labor) to a site of endangerment and finally, disconnect, as the speaker manifests as a split subject (with their lives "blocking the rear view" mirror). Indeed, she dissociates from her physical body, giving voice to a palpable separation. The swift movement between "Hurricane Isabel," "crumbling red brick," and "1970s standards" performs and enacts this disconnect, involving the reader in an impossible task of meaning making and creating unity from a discontinuous experience. "I found a pair of seagulls caught on two hooks of the same iridescent lure," she writes. Here, imagery mirrors the book's philosophical underpinnings.

As we traverse the "trauma," "fatal diseases," and "deal-breakers" that comprise the narrative, Womer shows us that not of these lexicons renders experience more faithfully than the last. Not the "chronic hunger" of the lyric interludes, nor the "categories" articulated in the more scientifically minded sections. Like Akbar, Womer uses silence, rupture and elision to call into question, and provocatively undermine, what is on the printed page.

Using the same stylistic repertoire, she gestures at the artifice of many conceptual models for understanding the physical body. Much like Akbar's provocative consideration of narrative and syntax, this argument is made through form and technique, rather than in the text proper. As Womer's hybrid sequence progresses, we are made to confront the varying levels of authority and credibility that we attribute to different registers and discourses, which, in this case, range from poetic imagery to medical jargon ("150 viruses, each assigned its own number").

"I wanted to be a mother but only on Sundays," Womer tell us. Throughout the collection, lyrical interludes like this one are juxtaposed with medical documents, patient questionnaires, and records of the senses. By transitioning between rhetorical modes in such a way, Womer suggests that the female voice is rarely accepted as a source of knowledge about the body, or a credible vehicle for an explanatory model. Indeed, Womer implies that facts about the body are often only seen as credible when they arrive in familiar forms, particularly those that populate the medical field and the biosciences. Yet it is in the silences, and the elisions, that these power dynamics become clear to the reader. It is in the apertures that the ethics of the text crystalize. As Womer herself tells us, "You didn't ask for a *miracle*, but got one anyway."

Rossouw's *Xamissa* continues Akbar's and Womer's exploration of what silence makes possible when articulating a philosophy of language. In the work's "Proloog," he notes that the title of this thought-provoking volume actually derives from linguistic accident:

> Perhaps it was here the urban legend emerged: "Camissa," we thought, meant "place of sweet waters" in the indigenous Khoe language. And the waters the urban legend speaks of have run from Table Mountain to the sea, under the city itself, since before the Dutch ships. An untrammeled toponym, from before the 1652 arrival of the Vereenigde Oostindische Compagnie (VOC), "Camissa" became a wellspring for the cultural reclamation I witnessed in newly democratic Cape Town. In the 2000s, Café Camissa shut down to make way for a real estate agency—a symptom.

Here meaning, and the task of translating, seem straightforward, but begin to unravel and refract over the course of Rossouw's introductory narrative. This anecdote frames the work beautifully, as the style of the writing skillfully performs this unraveling of narrative continuity.

Formally, the book begins with the semblance of wholeness, and the reader is borne from pristine prose paragraphs to the almost tangible documents of an archive. We are presented with the author's identity documents, and no accompanying information or caption. In an instant, the rhetorical situation of the work changes: the reader shifts from a passive recipient of meaning to an active agent in creating meaning. With that in mind, the space between texts and episodes in *Xamissa* is especially powerful. It is in these bright apertures, the liminal spaces within the text, that the laws of grammar, syntax and narrative no longer hold. In these brief pauses, the rules of the text, and the rules governing its language and narrative, can be entirely reconfigured.

*   *   *

"Heretofore unseen:/ a piece of census again/or a ship's manifest/ redacted with ash and/doubt," Rossouw writes. Like many passages in Xamissa, even the poetic line serves to amplify uncertainty. Just as the pause before "doubt" conveys even the narrator's trepidation, it is the silences in this work that are made to house the weight of history. Much like Akbar, Rossouw envisions silence as the center around which the book's poetics orbit. Just as *Calling a Wolf a Wolf* creates music out of all that cannot, and will not, be said aloud, *Xamissa* envisions the space between languages, histories, and temporal moments as an invitation, that "half-light" beckoning the reader inside what had once been a darkened room. As the book unfolds, its form – and the silences to which this experimentation give rise – become unruly, even disruptive, when considering the narrative conventions engaged by Akbar and Womer. Here, we are made to walk through the archive that accompanies any subject's life in language. Handwritten ledgers, official documents, and watermarks are juxtaposed with lines of poetry and lyric fragments. "I write the debris number C 2449 on the form/in pencil and wait for the ash in the half-light," Rossouw's speaker tells us.

In many ways, it is this movement between documents, "secrets," and "fire" that presents such a provocative challenge to what does exist on the printed page. Indeed, the transitions between different types of language, and the silence that fills the moments we spend in these liminal textual spaces, allows the reader to fully inhabit the archive in all of its indeterminacy, rather than a neatly structured master narrative. In other words, we encounter language – and the histories contained within it – in a nonhierarchical way. Like Womer's interrogation of medical jargon and the rhetoric of diagnosis, Rossouw erases the judgments, and the arbitrary valuations, that we impose upon different types of language and text. What's left is a "field on fire," a subversion of the politics surrounding the very documents he has gathered.

If silence is a gradual undoing, then the space between things makes visible that unraveling. It is the pauses between words that are most dangerous, as they hold the power to destabilize the text that surrounds them. Indeed, Rossouw's archival poetics reads as both homage and destruction, a lyric appreciation of the work silence can do (and undo).

*　　*　　*

When silence becomes a gradual undoing, an unraveling of certainty, there is a violence done by saying nothing. Womer, Akbar, and Rossouw undoubtedly destabilize many of the rules that govern our lives in language. At the same time, they do so with a true ethical sensibility, as their efforts to interrogate, and undermine, linguistic convention are borne out of a desire for a way of communicating that's more just and more true. For these three gifted poets, silence becomes a form of resistance, as well as a weapon and a relic of all that is holy. By interrogating the space between things, these poets have offered a philosophy of language where anything becomes possible. After all, it is in the liminal spaces that rules no longer hold. It is in the brief pauses between arias that it becomes possible to shift keys. As Rossouw observes in *Xamissa,* "I listen not in silence but in song, a form of interruption."

VOICE, ALTERITY, & APPROPRIATION: RECENT BOOKS BY DIANA KHO NGUYEN, MING HOLDEN, & CLAIRE MARIE STANCEK

The rich tradition linking poetic voice and alterity dates back to Homer, his epics, and his invocations to the muses to sing not *to* but *through* him. For many poets writing after him, the voices that inhabited literary texts were not their own, but instead an otherness that speaks through the poet, who is only a vessel. For H.D., this presence was the unconscious mind. Jack Spicer, on the other hand, described it as radio transmissions from outer space. For practitioners of collaborative writing, this otherness was instead a "third voice" that belongs to both of the collaborators and, at the same time, neither of them.

This conceptual framework, in which the poet is merely a conduit, challenges our beliefs about the ownership of language and literary texts in a way that is entirely provocative. The problem, however, is that responsibility and agency are entirely displaced. It becomes difficult to hold the writer responsible for words that are not their own. Three recent hybrid texts, however, skillfully combine a rich tradition that links poetic voice and alterity with a sense of social responsibility. Ming Holden's *Refuge,* Claire Marie Stancek's *Oil Spell,* an Diana Khoi Nguyen's *Ghost of* reframe this poetics of otherness as a form of activism and advocacy. For Holden, Stancek, and Nguyen, the otherness that speaks through the poet is not the unconscious mind, or radio transmissions, but rather, a collective voice, one persistently threatened with erasure.

For these three talented creative practitioners, the poet becomes a conduit for collective utterance. "Let us rise," Stancek declares in *Oil Spell,* as though speaking for the many disparate voices that will be unearthed, and placed in conversation, over the course of three polyphonic texts. And as these dispatches are "sent over many waters," the poetic text serves a documentary function, becoming a kind of ledger that resists the elisions of history. As Nguyen herself states, "Let's admit without embellishment what we do with each other."

*   *   *

In *Ghost of,* Nguyen presents narrative as a kind of conjuring. This is because all of speech is a shared endeavor, as one cannot form words without borrowing from a larger historical imagination. "Let me tell you a story about refugees," she writes midway through the collection. The speaker of Nguyen's poem serves as a vessel for these kinds of shared utterances, the book a ledger of all that has been elided by historical writing in a more traditional sense.

It is the space of poetry that offers an opportunity to close the gaps and fissures of more traditional histories. What is especially compelling about *Ghost of* is that this imaginative labor is made visible as Nguyen avails herself of a wide range of experimental forms. Histories and narratives appear with palpable "hollows," a "separate space" within each text that is left untouched. As the book unfolds, the reader discovers the missing piece - that "lost glove" – in close proximity to the "empty house," the "negative space" whose silhouette matches the shape of the language that "drifts" apart from the rest.

Nguyen writes, for example, in an untitled piece midway through the collection,

elemental	thinki
ng: a	n oce
an o	f sou
nd b	etwe
en w	aters

Presented with a smaller text circle on the facing page, Nguyen's formal choices speak to the ways that narrative, and the stories that make us ourselves, persist. They manifest against – and in spite of – erasure. "There is, you see, no shortage of gain and loss," she tells us. As the book unfolds, Nguyen shows us, tangibly and viscerally, how history's elisions shape – and circumscribe what is possible within – narrative. Her work poses what is essentially a profound question: how violence shapes – and in some ways makes possible – meaning, and how our lives would mean differently in a more just society.

A "poke berry," a gift. "Like some strange music, the world starts up again around us," Nguyen writes.

* * *

Holden's *Refuge* continues Nguyen's compelling exploration of collective utterance and social responsibility. Taking the form of a book-length lyric essay, Holden involves the reader in the shared narrative she creates through her evocative use of white space. In many ways, the discrete episodes that populate "Refuge," and the cavernous space between them, mirror the book's descriptions of disappearing traditions, stories, and ways of life. "No one positioned to inherit their space," she writes, "Simple."

Yet Holden complicates the seemingly "simple to describe" movements of history. "Violence and its aftermath disrupt the very systems of the mind," she tells us. Like Nguyen, she makes visible that "aftermath". At the same time, she places the reader in an active role, involving them in the task of rebuilding that "mosaic that might best honor" those who have been silenced.

What's more, Holden fearlessly and honestly confronts the ethical problems inherent in speaking for the other. She writes, for example, when discussing her work for "Survival Girls," a humanitarian organization that provided arts therapy to women,

140

Through my attempt to comprehend, the woman who is the referent, the woman violated, has been violated here.

Jacqueline.

[Jacqueline.]

[   ]

Here Holden raises what are essentially profound questions: Does the task of documentary poetics, and the shared histories that it often creates, empower, or does it take away agency? When does a shared history or collective utterance become an act of violence or appropriation? As Holden considers these complex ethical problems, her innovative approach to prose writing fully does justice to the complexity of her thinking. In *Refuge*, it is the white space, that "disturbance," that "trauma," that makes room for the other to speak.

*   *   *

Like Holden and Nguyen, Stancek envisions the act of conjuring as a kind of resistance. Drawing from many of the contemporary cultural moment's "dark energies," she interrogates the unique possibilities of poetry, and its specific artistic repertoire, for effecting social and ecological change. For Stancek, language is both a "lucif blast" and "illumination, a spark that floats down" to meet us. With that in mind, *Oil Spell* prompts us to rethink how language is used, bearing us from the utilitarian model we're familiar with to a linguistic structure without ownership, hierarchy, "solitude," or "abuse."

Stancek's anti-utilitarian approach to language manifests visibly in her presentation of the work on the page. By availing herself of a wide range of experimental forms, she jostles the hierarchies we associate with language and parts of speech, offering us only a "stray thing" and the "ravages of time." In many ways, this dismantling of hierarchies becomes an invitation to the reader, a pathway into the book's imaginative work. For example, she writes,

> Electrocution   and   airplane   strikes
> shepherds   BARNACLE   GOOSE
>   with guns ON THE GRASS UNDER
> CORVUS CORONE
>   THE SHADE OF SOME HIGH TREES
>   hurry into construction
>   NEAR THE RUINS
>   cones overturned

Here the audience is prompted to find meaning, and create cohesion from the "electrocution" and "ruins" of a séance. For some readers, the task may prove disconcerting, even discomfiting, yet this is precisely the point of the poet's formal experimentation.

In such a way, Stancek raises compelling questions about the nature of voice, alterity and appropriation: When does the poet have permission to serve as a conduit for the language of others? When does this divination become an appropriation of voice, narrative, and identity? And when is it an act of service, a form of against the erasures and elisions of history? As Stancek considers the ethical problems implicit in this kind of artistic endeavor, she offers us a poetics of conversation, dialogue, and response.

The text then, becomes merely a conduit, as the reader speaks through the fragments they are given. Stancek, like Holden and Nguyen, conjures through – and is conjured by – her accomplished and innovative approach to poetic craft. As Stancek herself writes, "full moon goodbye."

ACKNOWLEDGEMENTS

Thank you to the following magazines, where early versions of these essays first appeared:

Descant
The Kenyon Review
The Laurel Review
The Literary Review
The Los Angeles Review
The Los Angeles Review of Books
OmniVerse

Additional thanks to the Corportation of Yaddo, the Whiting Foundation, the American Academy in Rome, the Helene Wurlitzer Foundation, the Virginia Center for the Creative Arts, and the Dorland Mountain Arts Colony for their generous support during the time these essays were written.

ABOUT THE AUTHOR

Kristina Marie Darling is the author of thirty-two books, including *Look to Your Left: The Poetics of Spectacle* (Akron Poetry Series, forthcoming in 2020); *Veronica in Cyberspace: Notes on Love + Light* (Eyewear Publishing, forthcoming in 2019); *Violence, Rage, & Disbelief: A Woman's Guide to the Kavanaugh Appointment* (Eyewear Publishing, forthcoming in 2019); *Je Suis L'Autre: Essays & Interrogations* (C&R Press, 2017), which was named one of the "Best Books of 2017" by *The Brooklyn Rail;* and *DARK HORSE: Poems* (C&R Press, 2018), which received a starred review in *Publishers Weekly.* Her work has been recognized with three residencies at Yaddo, where she has held both the Martha Walsh Pulver Residency for a Poet and the Howard Moss Residency in Poetry; a Fundación Valparaíso fellowship; a Hawthornden Castle Fellowship, funded by the Heinz Foundation; an artist-in-residence position at Cité Internationale des Arts in Paris; four residencies at the American Academy in Rome; two grants from the Whiting Foundation; a joint award from the Wallace Stegner Estate and the Eastend Arts Council; a Morris Fellowship in the Arts; and the Dan Liberthson Prize from the Academy of American Poets, which she received on three separate occasions, among many other awards and honors. Her poems appear in *The Harvard Review, Poetry International, New American Writing, Nimrod, Passages North, The Mid-American Review,* and on the Academy of American Poets' website, Poets.org. She has published essays in *Agni, Ploughshares, The Gettysburg Review, Gulf Coast, The Green Mountains Review, The Iowa Review, The Literary Review,* and numerous other magazines. Kristina currently serves as Editor-in-Chief of Tupelo Press and *Tupelo Quarterly,* an opinion columnist at *The Los Angeles Review of Books,* a contributing writer at *Publishers Weekly,* a staff blogger at *The Kenyon Review,* and a freelance book critic at *The New York Times Book Review.*

C&R PRESS TITLES

NONFICTION

Women in the Literary Landscape by Doris Weatherford, et al
Credo: An Anthology of Manifestos & Sourcebook for Creative Writing
by Rita Banerjee and Diana Norma Szokolyai

FICTION

Last Tower to Heaven by Jacob Paul
No Good, Very Bad Asian by Lelund Cheuk
Surrendering Appomattox by Jacob M. Appel
Made by Mary by Laura Catherine Brown
Ivy vs. Dogg by Brian Leung
While You Were Gone by Sybil Baker
Cloud Diary by Steve Mitchell
Spectrum by Martin Ott
That Man in Our Lives by Xu Xi

SHORT FICTION

Notes From the Mother Tongue by An Tran
The Protester Has Been Released by Janet Sarbanes

ESSAY AND CREATIVE NONFICTION

In the Room of Persistent Sorry by Kristina Marie Darling
the internet is for real by Chris Campanioni
Immigration Essays by Sybil Baker
Je suis l'autre: Essays and Interrogations by Kristina Marie Darling
Death of Art by Chris Campanioni

POETRY

A Family is a House by Dustin Pearson
The Miracles by Amy Lemmon
Banjo's Inside Coyote by Kelli Allen
Objects in Motion by Jonathan Katz
My Stunt Double by Travis Denton
Lessons in Camoflauge by Martin Ott
Millenial Roost by Dustin Pearson
Dark Horse by Kristina Marie Darling
All My Heroes are Broke by Ariel Francisco
Holdfast by Christian Anton Gerard
Ex Domestica by E.G. Cunningham
Like Lesser Gods by Bruce McEver
Notes from the Negro Side of the Moon by Earl Braggs
Imagine Not Drowning by Kelli Allen
Notes to the Beloved by Michelle Bitting
Free Boat: Collected Lies and Love Poems by John Reed
Les Fauves by Barbara Crooker
Tall as You are Tall Between Them by Annie Christain

CPSIA information can be obtained
at www.ICGtesting.com
Printed in the USA
FSHW010851180319
56389FS